# SOCIAL ECOLOGY
# AND THE
# ROJAVA REVOLUTION

# INTERNATIONALIST COMMUNE OF ROJAVA

## IN COOPERATION WITH THE DEMOCRATIC SELF-GOVERNANCE OF NORTHERN SYRIA

First published in London, 2022 by Dog Section Press
and Internationalist Commune of Rojava
Printed by Calverts Ltd., a worked-owned cooperative

ISBN 9781916036598

Graphic design by Matt Bonner - revoltdesign.org
Dog Section Press logo by Want Some Studio

# SOCIAL ECOLOGY AND THE ROJAVA REVOLUTION

Compiled by
## INTERNATIONALIST COMMUNE OF ROJAVA

Illustrated by
## MATT BONNER

# CONTENTS

---

# LIST OF ILLUSTRATIONS

---

A quote by Murray Bookchin from *Remaking Society: Pathways to a Green Future*.

A tribute to the village of Jinwar in Rojava. Jinwar is a community established in 2016 for women to live and work together, inspired by the three basic principles of the Kurdish freedom movement: democracy, ecology and women's liberation. 'Jin', the Kurdish word for 'woman' and 'war' meaning 'space/land.'

ANKARA

T U R K E Y

BAKU

ROJAV

SYRIA

DAMASCUS

## MAP OF
# KURDISTAN

The distrubution of the Kurdish
population in the Middle East.

This book has been typeset by
SALT PUBLISHING LIMITED
using Granjon, a font designed by George W. Jones
for the British branch of the Linotype
company in the United Kingdom. It has been
manufactured using Holmen Book Cream
65gsm paper, and printed and bound by Clays
Limited in Bungay, Suffolk, Great Britain.

CROMER
GREAT BRITAIN
MMXXV

N

TURKEY

KOBANI

TELL ABYAD

AFRIN

ALEPPO

SYRIA

MAP OF
# ROJAVA
Autonomous Administration
of North and East Syria

Source: Rojava Information Centre, May 2020

QAMISHLO

DÉRIKA HEMKO

SERÊ KANÎYÊ

AL-HASAKAH

ROJAVA

IRAQ

QQA

Kurdish-led Syrian
Democratic Forces
and/or Asayish

Turkish armed
forces and Turkish-
controlled Syrian
national army

Syrian Arab Army

# GLOSSARY

---

## DEMOCRATIC CONFEDERALISM

---

Democratic Confederalism is an egalitarian form of government that draws upon social ecology and libertarian municipalism, concentrating power at the most local level (the "commune," or a group of families/homes). A network of elected administrative councils links communities together and allows citizens to manage the affairs of their neighborhood with a high degree of autonomy.

## JINEOLOGY

---

Jineology, or women's science, is a framework of radical feminist analysis developed by Abdullah Öcalan and the Kurdish freedom movement since 2008. It is based on the concrete experiences of Kurdish women facing both patriarchal and colonial oppression and criticises how the monotheistic religions, the nation-state and capitalism have monopolised all forms of power in the hands of men. Jineology seeks to develop an alternative methodology for the existing social sciences that stands in contrast to androcentric knowledge systems, and restore women's central place in society.

## KURDISTAN

Kurdistan is the region wherein the Kurds form a majority population and the Kurdish culture, languages, and national identity have historically been based. Kurdistan generally comprises the following four regions: Bakur (Northern Kurdistan) in southeastern Turkey, Rojhilat (Eastern Kurdistan) in northwestern Iran, Basur (Southern Kurdistan) in northern Iraq and Rojava (Western Kurdistan) in northern Syria.

## LIBERTARIAN MUNICIPALISM

Libertarian municipalism is a political program developed by Communalist and social ecologist theorist Murray Bookchin to create democratic citizens' assemblies in villages, towns and urban neighborhoods that have elected recallable, accountable delegates who act as the voice of their assemblies. The assemblies in these free municipalities join together to replace the state with a directly democratic confederation that can govern on an ever-larger scale without resorting to traditional "representative" politics.

# ROJAVA

---

Rojava, the Autonomous Administration of North and East Syria (NES), is made up of several self-governing regions: Afrin, Jazeera (also called Cizre), Raqqa, Tabqa, Deir al-Zour, Manbij, and Euphrates. Though it began as a mostly-Kurdish autonomous zone in a region left vacant during the Syrian Civil War, Rojava is now a pluralistic society comprised of many ethnic groups. The word Rojava means "West," as in Western Kurdistan.

# SOCIAL ECOLOGY

---

Beginning with the premise that the domination of nature is a product of the domination of human by human, social ecology advocates a complete reordering of society to eliminate all forms of hierarchy. Social ecology envisions a moral economy that moves beyond scarcity and hierarchy toward a world that reharmonises human communities with the natural world while celebrating diversity, creativity, and freedom. As part of its reconstructive and transformative outlook on social and environmental issues, social ecology promotes a directly democratic, confederal politics based on local assemblies that its founder, Murray Bookchin, described as Libertarian Municipalism or Communalism. These ideas influenced Kurdish leader Abdullah Öcalan, who adapted them for the Middle East under the name Democratic Confederalism.

ŞEHÎD NAMIRIN
MARTYRS NEVER DIE

The freedom to face the challenges of building an ecological society in Northern Syria is, first and foremost, due to the many martyrs of this revolution.

Without their struggle, there would be no liberated ground in Rojava on which to sow the seeds of ecological living.

This book is dedicated to them.

JIN JÎYAN
AZADÎ

WOMEN LIFE FREEDOM

# INTRODUCTION

## Debbie Bookchin

---

I t has become impossible to deny the deep ecological crisis imperilling our planet. Poisoned air, dying coral reefs, scorching heat, wildfires, and the flood waters of "super storms" that pummel us as global temperatures rise – these are just a few of the many environmental traumas bearing witness to the immense destruction of the ecosystems of Earth.

For decades, the accepted response has been to silo these environmental degradations, treating them as isolated problems and attempting to solve them with piecemeal responses. Governments ban certain chemicals; well-meaning scientists suggest we deploy smarter technology; advocacy groups push for "greener" consumer products. Only recently has the public discussion finally acknowledged the obvious: our ecological crisis has a deeper, structural basis and we cannot save the planet if we do not address this head on.

Murray Bookchin was the original exponent of this viewpoint. Bookchin began predicting a coming ecological crisis in his writings beginning in the early 1960s, and after a thorough analysis concluded that the ecological crisis cannot be separated from the social crisis. In a series of books and essays over the next four decades, Bookchin laid out his central theme: at its root, our ecological crisis is not just a crisis of capitalism, important as that may be. More fundamentally, it is a crisis of hierarchy and domination, whose effects are readily seen in the deep divisions in wealth, status, and well-being that permeate society today.

The many forms of hierarchy we experience in society – based on age, gender, ethnicity, sexual orientation, religion, ableness, and economic status, among others – are projected onto the natural world in a rapacious, exploitive attitude toward nature. As Bookchin wrote in 1964, "The imbalances man has produced in the natural world are caused by the imbalances he has produced in the social world." He frames the problem even more succinctly in an essay from 1986 that is included in this volume: "All of our present ecological problems originate in deep-seated social problems."

Bookchin used the expression social ecology to capture these concepts. Kurdish leader Abdullah Öcalan, whose work is also featured in this volume, breathed new life into Bookchin's ideas when he made social ecology one of the main pillars guiding the Kurdish freedom movement. Like Bookchin, Öcalan presents a searing critique of how social imbalances and hierarchy, in particular the oppression of women, are manifesting themselves in our ecological crisis. "As with the problem of women's freedom," Öcalan observes, "the patriarchal and statist understanding of power also contributes to the fact that ecological problems have been delayed for so long and have still not been solved properly." Öcalan's philosophy, Democratic Confederalism – built on the pillars of women's rights, social ecology, and direct democracy – undergirds the Rojava Revolution and has made it an important example for how to build an ecological, egalitarian society from the ground up.

While the other two pillars of the Rojava Revolution – direct democracy and women's liberation – have received close attention because of the enormous impact they have had on everyday life in Rojava, social ecology is also a critically important backdrop to the transformation underway in the region. This volume, *Social Ecology and the Rojava Revolution*, provides an excellent introduction to the concept of social ecology and why it plays such an important role in the liberatory society being built by the five million Kurds, Arabs, Assyrian Christians, Yczidis, and people of other ethnicities who together live and govern the Autonomous Administration of North and East Syria, more informally known as Rojava.

Social ecology is not just a critical philosophy: it is a reconstructive one as well. It insists that we completely rethink our relationships to each other and to the natural world. It asks us to look to nature for a model of how social relations can be reimagined so that all forms of hierarchy are eliminated in favour of horizontal, ecological models, where every species plays a role in maintaining ecosystem balance.

Social ecology shows us that the mechanisms at work in a healthy ecosystem – diversity, non-hierarchy, symbiosis built on complexity – are the very elements necessary to restore social relations in order to achieve norms that foster mutual aid and sustainability, rather than competition and strife. Bookchin and Öcalan understood that these are the values that would allow us to achieve a truly ethical society and heal our relationships with each other and nature. As Öcalan states in his essay included in this book: "No social system that is not in harmony with nature can claim rationality and morality for itself."

How do we create an ecological, ethical society? We can begin by asking fundamental questions such as: What is nature? What is humanity's place in nature? What is the thrust of natural evolution? And ultimately, of course: What would a rational relationship between human beings and the natural world consist of? In reconceptualising our relationship with nature, we can make some basic observations.

First, the prevailing notion in Western philosophy, including Marxism, that nature is somehow "hostile" or "stingy" or based simply on the survival of the fittest, doesn't conform to reality. Darwin bequeathed to us a notion of nature as one of rivalries and competition. As a result, for too long we have superimposed categories of hierarchy on the natural world when, in fact, stable ecological systems are those that are symbiotic, non-hierarchical, and diverse.

Social ecology frees nature from these anthropocentric views – trappings imposed on it by a cutthroat capitalist mentality.

Social ecology observes nature as directed and striving for ever-greater diversity. This differentiation and symbiosis encourages stability in an ecosystem; symbiosis fosters the survival of plants and animals far more than the notion of pure competition would allow. As such, we can begin to see a thrust in natural evolution toward diversity, individuation, creativity, and, in the form of human beings with their complex nervous systems and high functioning brains, toward self-consciousness and reason.

Second, inasmuch as human beings emerge from nature, these concepts of selfhood, reason, and freedom should not be seen as antagonistic to the natural world, but rather an expression of nature in its most advanced form. The German philosopher Johann Gottlieb Fichte called human beings "nature rendered self-conscious." Bookchin suggests we are nature rendered *potentially* self-conscious, inasmuch as we have yet to behave in the fully rational fashion that would exhibit true self-consciousness. Ocalan observes, "Philosophy defines the human being as 'nature becoming aware of itself.' The human being is basically the most developed part of nature." This means that human beings have the ability and the responsibility to intervene rationally in nature and society to enhance stability and freedom.

This striving toward reason and freedom is a potentiality within nature – not a law of nature, to be sure, but a *possibility* that exists, which human beings alone have the capacity to bring to fruition. Thus, social ecology is fundamentally a philosophy of potentialities, of development, of "being" as "becoming." An immanent striving for realisation doesn't mean a predetermined outcome. As Bookchin says: it is a message of freedom, not of necessity.

This means that we can think of principles like complementarity and participation to describe not only the mutualistic interactions of animals and plants, but of people who, ever more differentiated, bring these principles into the social arena, opening up new evolutionary horizons in nature and society. If the thrust of nature is toward ever greater diversity and freedom, we as human beings must bring the fullest realisation of this tendency to fruition in non-hierarchical, egalitarian societies that foster variation, differentiation, and creativity.

---

As the diverse essays in this book illustrate, Rojava, with its emphasis on direct democracy, social ecology, and women's liberation, exemplifies the realisation of the unique potential of human beings to create rational, ecological societies that enhance freedom for all. Readers will find not only the theoretical foundations of social ecology, but importantly, glimpses of its practice in Rojava and in the women's movement that model how we can organise society in non-hierarchical ways that foster a healthy non-exploitive relationship to nature.

Like the French utopian thinker Charles Fourier before him, Öcalan observed that a society cannot be deemed free unless women are free. Indeed, the measure of whether we will have achieved a truly free, rational, and ecological society will be whether we eliminate capitalism, the state, and *all* hierarchies. In this project, the people of Rojava have provided the world with a vibrant example. Hopefully we will have the courage to follow their lead.

———————

**Debbie Bookchin**, a longtime journalist and author, is the editor of several books by her father, the social ecologist Murray Bookchin, including *The Modern Crisis*, *The Philosophy of Social Ecology*, and *Remaking Society*. She co-edited his posthumous book of essays, *The Next Revolution: Popular Assemblies and the Promise of Direct Democracy* (2015) and is cofounder of the U.S.-based Rojava solidarity group, Emergency Committee for Rojava.

# THE RETURN TO SOCIAL ECOLOGY

## Abdullah Öcalan

A social 'consciousness' that lacks ecological consciousness will inevitably corrupt and disintegrate. Just as the system has led the social into chaos, so has the environment begun to send out S.O.S. signals in the form of life-threatening catastrophes. Cancer-like cities, polluted air, the perforated ozone layer, the rapidly accelerating extinction of animal and plant species, the destruction of forests, the pollution of water by waste, piling up mountains of rubbish and unchecked growth have driven the environment into chaos and insurrection. It's all about maximum profit, regardless of how many cities, factories, transportation, synthetic materials, polluted air and water our planet can handle.

This negative development is not fated. It is the result of an unbalanced use of science and technology in the hands of power. It would be wrong to hold science and technology responsible for this process. Science and technology in themselves are not to blame. They function according to the forces of the social system. Just as they can destroy nature, so they can heal it. The problem is exclusively a social one. There is a great contradiction between the level of science and technology and the standard of living of the overwhelming majority of people. This situation is the result of the interests of a minority that has control over science and technology. In a democratic and free society, however, science and technology will play an ecological role.

Ecology itself is also a science. It examines the relationship of society to its environment. Although it is still a very young science, it will play a leading role in overcoming the contradiction between society and nature, together with all other sciences. The environmental consciousness that has already been developed in places will make a revolutionary leap forward through ecology understood in this way. The bond between the communal primitive society and nature is like the bond between child and mother. Nature is understood as something alive. The golden rule of the religion of this time was not to do anything against it in order not to be punished by it.

The natural religion is the religion of the communal primitive society. There is no contradiction to nature, no anomaly in the emergence of society. Philosophy defines the human being as "nature becoming aware of itself." The human being is basically the most developed part of nature. This proves the unnaturalness of this social system, which puts the most developed part of nature in contradiction to it. The fact that this social system has turned the human, who enthusiastically united himself with nature in feasts, into such a plague for nature shows that it is itself the plague. The holistic nature of the human and the natural environment does not only refer to economic and social issues. It is also an indispensable philosophical passion to understand nature. This is actually based on reciprocity. Nature proves its great curiosity and creative power by becoming human. The human being, on the other hand, recognises itself by understanding nature. It is remarkable that the Sumerian word for freedom, "Amargi," means return to the mother – nature. Between human beings and nature there is a quasi-love relationship. This is a great love story. To destroy this love is, religiously speaking, a mortal sin. Because you cannot create a greater sense of meaning than this one.

No social system that is not in harmony with nature can claim rationality and morality for itself. Therefore, the system that is most at odds with nature will also be the least developed in terms of rationality and morality. As can be seen from this brief definition of the contradiction between the capitalist social system and its present chaotic state and the catastrophic destruction of the environment, it is a dialectical relationship. The fundamental contradiction to nature can only be overcome by turning away from the system. It cannot be solved by environmental protection movements alone. On the other hand, an ecological society also requires a moral change. The amorality of capitalism can only be overcome by an ecological approach. The connection between morality and conscience demands an empathetic and sympathetic spirituality. This in turn only makes sense if it is based on ecological competence. Ecology means friendship with nature, belief in natural religion. In this respect ecology stands for a renewed, conscious and enlightened union into a natural, organic society.

The practical problems of an ecological way of life are quite topical. One of the tasks of activists is to expand the many existing organisations in every respect and to make them an integral part of democratic society. This also includes solidarity with the feminist movements. One of the most important activities in democratisation is the promotion and organisation of environmental awareness. Just as there once was a pronounced class or national consciousness, we must create an awareness of democracy and the environment through intensive campaigns. Whether we are talking about animal rights, the protection of forests or reforestation, such actions, if carried out properly, are indispensable elements of social activism. People who have no feeling for the biological can only have a disturbed social feeling.

Those who perceive the relationship between the two can feel true with all their senses. Nature, which has so far been plundered and exposed, must and will witness a great struggle to restore its cover of flora and fauna. The forest will have to be given a chance again. "Great patriotism means reforestation and planting trees." This is a valuable slogan.

Those who do not love and protect animals will also not be able to protect and love humans. A social "consciousness" that lacks ecological consciousness will inevitably corrupt and disintegrate, as was seen with real-socialism. Ecological consciousness is a fundamental ideological consciousness. It resembles a bridge between philosophy and morality. A policy that promises salvation from the current crisis can only lead to a real social system if it is ecological. As with the problem of women's freedom, the patriarchal and statist understanding of power also contributes to the fact that ecological problems have been delayed for so long and have still not been solved properly. If ecology and feminism continue to develop, the patriarchal and statist system becomes completely out of balance.

The true struggle for democracy and socialism will only be complete when it takes up the cause of women's freedom and nature's salvation. Only such a complete struggle for a new social system can meaningfully lead to a way out of the current chaos.

---

**Abdullah Öcalan** actively led the Kurdish liberation struggle as the head of the PKK from its foundation in 1978 until his abduction by the Turkish state on 15 February 1999. He is still regarded as a leading strategist and the most important political representative of the Kurdish freedom movement. Under isolation conditions at Imrali Island Prison, Öcalan authored more than ten books that have revolutionised Kurdish politics.

This text is an excerpt from Abdullah Öcalan's defence pamphlet Bir Halkı Savunmak (Beyond State, Power and Violence).

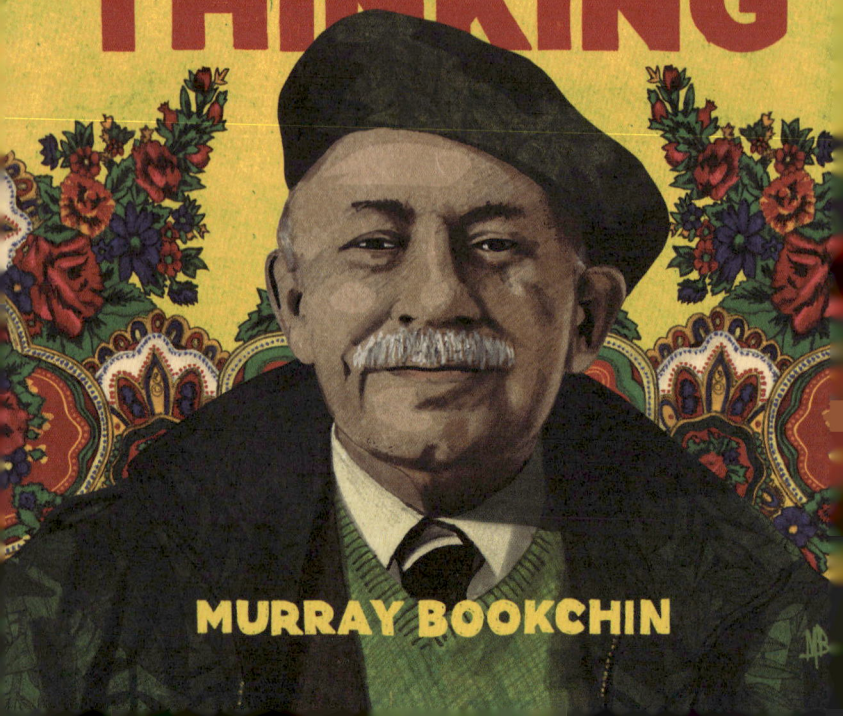

THE ASSUMPTION THAT WHAT CURRENTLY EXISTS MUST NECESSARILY EXIST IS THE ACID THAT CORRODES ALL VISIONARY THINKING

MURRAY BOOKCHIN

# WHAT IS
# SOCIAL ECOLOGY?

## Murray Bookchin

---

Social ecology is based on the conviction that nearly all of our present ecological problems originate in deep-seated social problems. It follows, from this view, that these ecological problems cannot be understood, let alone solved, without a careful understanding of our existing society and the irrationalities that dominate it. To make this point more concrete: economic, ethnic, cultural, and gender  conflicts, among many others, lie at the core of the most serious ecological dislocations we face today – apart, to be sure, from those that are produced by natural catastrophes. The massive oil spills that have occurred over the past two decades, the extensive deforestation of tropical forest and magnificent ancient trees in temperate areas, and vast hydroelectric projects that flood places where people live, to cite only a few problems, are sobering reminders that the real battleground on which the ecological future of the planet will be decided is clearly a social one, particularly between corporate power and the long-range interests of humanity as a whole.

Indeed, to separate ecological problems from social problems – or even to play down or give only token recognition to their crucial relationship – would be to grossly misconstrue the sources of the growing environmental crisis. In effect, the way human beings deal with each other as social beings is crucial to addressing the ecological crisis. Unless we clearly recognise this, we will fail to see that the hierarchical mentality and class relationships that so thoroughly permeate society are what has given rise to the very idea of dominating the natural world.

Unless we realise that the present market society, structured around the brutally competitive imperative of "grow or die," is a thoroughly impersonal, self-operating mechanism, we will falsely tend to blame other phenomena – such as technology or population growth – for growing environmental dislocations. We will ignore their root causes, such as trade for profit, industrial expansion for its own sake, and the identification of progress with corporate self-interest. In short, we will tend to focus on the *symptoms* of a grim social pathology rather than on the pathology itself, and our efforts will be directed toward limited goals whose attainment is more cosmetic than curative.

## NATURE AND SOCIETY

To escape from this profit-oriented image of ecology, let us begin with some basics – namely, by asking what society and the natural world actually are. Among the many definitions of *nature* that have been formulated over time, the one that has the most affinity with social ecology is rather elusive and often difficult to grasp because understanding and articulating it requires a certain way of thinking – one that stands *at odds* with what is popularly called "linear thinking." This "nonlinear" or organic way of thinking is developmental rather than analytical, or in more technical terms, it is dialectical rather than instrumental. It conceives the natural world as a *developmental process*, rather than the beautiful vistas we see from a mountaintop or images fixed on the backs of picture postcards. Such vistas and images of nonhuman nature are basically static and immobile. As we gaze over a landscape, to be sure, our attention may momentarily be arrested by the soaring flight of a hawk, or the bolting leap of a deer, or the low-slung shadowy lope of a coyote. But what we are really witnessing in such cases is the mere kinetics of physical motion, caught in the frame of an essentially static image of the scene before our eyes. Such static images deceive us into believing in the "eternality" of single moments in nature.

But nonhuman nature is more than a scenic view, and as we examine it with some care, we begin to sense that it is basically an evolving and unfolding phenomenon, a richly fecund, even dramatic development that is forever changing. I mean to define nonhuman nature precisely as an evolving process, as the *totality*, in fact, of its evolution. Nature, so concerned, encompasses the development from the inorganic into the organic, and from the less differentiated and relatively limited world of unicellular organisms into that of multicellular ones equipped with simple, then complex, and in time fairly intelligent neural apparatuses that allow them to make innovative choices. Finally, the acquisition of warm-bloodedness gives to organisms the astonishing flexibility to exist in the most demanding climatic environments.

This vast drama of nonhuman nature is in every respect stunning and wondrous. Its evolution is marked by increasing subjectivity and flexibility and by increasing differentiation that makes an organism more adaptable to new environmental challenges and opportunities and that better equips living beings (specifically human beings) to *alter* their environment to meet their own needs rather than merely adapt to environmental changes. One may speculate that the potentiality of matter itself – the ceaseless interactivity of atoms in forming new chemical combinations to produce ever more complex molecules, amino acids, proteins and, under suitable conditions, elementary life-forms – is inherent in inorganic nature. Or one may decide quite matter-of-factly that the "struggle for existence" or the "survival of the fittest" explains why increasingly subjective and more flexible beings are capable of addressing environmental change more effectively than are less subjective and flexible beings. But the simple fact remains that these evolutionary dramas did occur, indeed the evidence is carved in stone in the fossil record. That nonhuman nature is this record, this history, this developmental or evolutionary process, is a very sobering fact that cannot be ignored without ignoring reality itself.

Conceiving nonhuman nature as its own interactive evolution rather than as a mere scenic vista has profound implications – ethical as well as biological – for ecologically minded people. Human beings embody, at least potentially, attributes of nonhuman development that place them squarely within organic evolution. They are not "natural aliens," to use Neil Evernden's phrase, strong exotics, phylogenetic deformities that, owing to their tool-making capacities, "cannot evolve *with* an ecosystem anywhere." Nor are they "intelligent fleas," to use the language of Gaian theorists who believe that the earth ("Gaia") is one living organism. These untenable disjunctions between humanity and the evolutionary process are as superficial as they are potentially misanthropic. Humans are highly intelligent, indeed, very self-conscious primates, which is to say that they have emerged – not diverged – from a long evolution of vertebrate life-forms into mammalian and finally primate life-forms. They are a product of a significant evolutionary trend toward intellectuality, self-awareness, will, intentionality, and expressiveness, be it in verbal or in body language.

Human beings belong to a natural continuum, no less than their primate ancestors and mammals in general. To depict them as "aliens" that have no place or pedigree in natural evolution, or to see them essentially as an infestation that parasitises the planet the way fleas parasitise dogs and cats, is not only bad ecology but bad thinking. Lacking any sense of process, this kind of thinking – regrettably so commonplace among ethicists – radically divides the nonhuman from the human. Indeed, to the degree environmental thinkers romanticise nonhuman nature as wilderness and see it as more authentically "natural" than the works of humans, they freeze nonhuman nature as a circumscribed domain in which human innovation, foresight, and creativity have no place and offer no possibilities.

The truth is that human beings not only belong in nature, they are products of a long, natural evolutionary process. Their seemingly "unnatural" activities – like the development of technology and science, the formation of mutable social institutions, highly symbolic forms of communication and aesthetic sensibilities, and the creation of towns and cities – all would have been impossible without the large array of physical human attributes that have been aeons in the making, be they the large human brain or the bipedal motion that frees human hands for making tools and carrying food. In many respects, human traits are enlargements of nonhuman traits that have been evolving over the ages. Increasing care for the young, cooperation, the substitution of mentally guided behavior for largely instinctive behavior – all are present more keenly in human behaviour. Among humans, as opposed to nonhuman beings, these traits are developed sufficiently to reach a degree of elaboration and integration that yields cultures, comprising institutions of families, bands, tribes, hierarchies, economic classes, and the state – in short, highly mutable societies for which there is no precedent in the nonhuman world, unless the genetically programmed behavior of insects is to be regarded as social. In fact, the emergence and development of human society has been a continual process of shedding instinctive behavioral traits and of clearing a new terrain for potentially rational behavior.

Human beings always remain rooted in their biological evolutionary history, which we may call "first nature," but they produce a characteristically human social nature of their own, which we may call "second nature." Far from being unnatural, human second nature is eminently a creation of organic evolution's first nature. To write second nature out of nature as a whole, or indeed to minimise it, is to ignore the creativity of natural evolution itself and to view it one-sidedly. If "true" evolution embodies itself simply in creatures like grizzly bears, wolves, and whales – generally, animals that *people* find aesthetically pleasing or relatively intelligent – then human beings are de-natured. Such views, whether they see human beings as "aliens" or as "fleas," essentially place them outside the self-organising thrust of natural evolution toward increasing subjectivity and flexibility. The more enthusiastic proponents of this de-naturing of humanity may see human beings as existing apart from nonhuman evolution, as a "freaking," as Paul Shepard put it, of the evolutionary process. Others simply avoid the problem of clarifying humanity's unique place in natural evolution by promiscuously putting human beings on a par with beetles in terms of their "intrinsic worth." The "either/or" propositional thinking that produces such obfuscations either separates the social from the organic altogether or flippantly makes it disappear into the organic, resulting in an inexplicable dualism at one extreme or a naïve reductionism at the other. The dualistic approach, with its quasi-theological premise that the world was "made" for human use, is saddled with the name *anthropocentrism*, while the reductionist approach, with its almost meaningless notion of a "biocentric democracy," is saddled with the name *biocentrism*.

The bifurcation of the human from the nonhuman reflects a failure to think organically or to approach evolutionary phenomena with an evolutionary way of thought. Needless to say, if nature were no more than a scenic vista, then mere metaphoric and poetic descriptions of it might suffice to replace systematic thinking about it. But *nature is the history of nature*, an evolutionary process that is going on to one degree or another under our very eyes, and as such, we dishonour it by thinking of it in anything but a processual way. That is to say, we require a way of thinking that recognises that "what is," as it seems to lie before our eyes, is always developing into "what is not," that it is engaged in a continual self-organising process in which past and present, along a richly differentiated but shared continuum, give rise to a new potentiality for an ever-richer degree of *wholeness*. Life, clearly in its human form, becomes open-endedly innovative and transcends its relatively narrow capacity to adapt only to a pregiven set of environmental conditions. As V. Gordon Childe once put it, "Man makes himself; he is not preset to survive by his genetic makeup."

By the same token, a processual, organic, and dialectical way of thinking has little difficulty in locating and explaining the emergence of the social out of the biological, of second nature out of first nature. To truly *know* and be able to give interpretive *meaning* to the social issues and ideas so arranged, we should want to know how each one derived from the other and what its part is in an overall development. What, in fact, is meant by "decentralisation," and how, in the history of human society, does it derive from or give rise to centralisation? We need processual thinking to comprehend processual realities, if we are to gain some sense of *direction* – practical as well as theoretical – in addressing our ecological problems.

Social ecology seems to stand alone, at present, in calling for an organic, developmental way of thinking out problems that are basically organic and developmental in character. The very definition of the natural world as a development indicates the need for organic thinking, as does the derivation of human from nonhuman nature – a derivation from which we can draw far-reaching conclusions for the development of an ecological ethics that in turn can provide serious guidelines for the solution of our ecological problems.

Social ecology calls upon us to see that the natural world and the social are interlinked by evolution into one nature that consists of two differentiations: first or biotic nature, and second or social nature. Social nature and biotic nature share an evolutionary potential for greater subjectivity and flexibility. Second nature is the way in which human beings, as flexible, highly intelligent primates, inhabit and *alter* the natural world. That is to say, people create an environment that is most suitable for their mode of existence. In this respect, second nature is no different from the environment that every animal, depending upon its abilities, partially creates as well as primarily adapts to – the biophysical circumstances or ecocommunity in which it must live. In principle, on this very simple level, human beings are doing nothing that differs from the survival activities of nonhuman beings, be it building beaver dams or digging gopher holes.

But the environmental changes that human beings produce are profoundly different from those produced by nonhuman beings. Humans act upon their environments with considerable technical *foresight*, however lacking that foresight may be in ecological ideals. Animals adapt to the world around them; human beings innovate through thought and social labor. For better or worse, they alter the natural world to meet their needs and desires – not because they are perverse, but because they have evolved quite naturally over the ages to do so. Their cultures are rich in knowledge, experience, cooperation, and conceptual intellectuality; however, they have been sharply divided against themselves at many points of their development, through conflicts between groups, classes, nation-states, and even city-states. Nonhuman beings generally live in ecological niches, their behavior guided primarily by instinctive drives and conditioned reflexes. Human societies are "bonded" together by *institutions* that change radically over centuries. Nonhuman communities are notable for their general fixity, by their clearly preset, often genetically imprinted rhythms. Human communities are guided in part by ideological factors and are subject to changes conditioned by those factors. Nonhuman communities are generally tied together by genetically rooted instinctive factors – to the extent that these communities exist at all.

Hence human beings, emerging from an organic evolutionary process, initiate, by the sheer force of their biological and survival needs, a social evolutionary development that clearly involves their organic evolutionary process. Owing to their naturally endowed intelligence, powers of communication, capacity for institutional organisation, and relative freedom from instinctive behavior, they refashion their environment – as do nonhuman beings – to the full extent that their biological equipment allows. This equipment makes it possible for them to engage not only in social life but in social development. It is not so much that human beings, in principle, behave differently from animals or are inherently more problematical in a strictly ecological sense, as it is that the social development by which they grade out of their biological development often becomes more problematical for themselves and nonhuman life. How these problems emerge, the ideologies they produce, the extent to which they contribute to biotic evolution or abort it, and the damage they inflict on the planet as a whole lie at the very heart of the modern ecological crisis. Second nature as it exists today, far from marking the fulfillment of human potentialities, is riddled by contradictions, antagonisms, and conflicting interests that have distorted humanity's unique capacities for development. Its future prospects encompass both the danger of tearing down the biosphere and, given the struggle to achieve an ecological society, the capacity to provide an entirely new ecological dispensation.

## SOCIAL HIERARCHY AND DOMINATION

How, then, did the social emerge from the biological? We have good reason to believe that as biological facts such as kin lineage, gender distinctions, and age differences were slowly institutionalised, their uniquely social dimension was initially quite egalitarian. Later this development acquired an oppressive hierarchical and then an exploitative class form. The lineage or blood tie in early prehistory obviously formed the organic basis of the family. Indeed, it joined together groups of families into bands, clans, and tribes, through either intermarriage or fictive forms of descent, thereby forming the earliest social horizon of our ancestors. More than in other mammals, the simple biological facts of human reproduction and the protracted maternal care of the human infant tended to knit siblings together and produced a strong sense of solidarity and group inwardness. Men, women, and their children were socialised by means of a *fairly* stable family life, based on mutual obligation and an expressed affinity that was often sanctified by initiation ceremonies and marital vows of one kind or another.

Human beings who were outside the family and all its elaborations into bands, clans, tribes, and the like, were regarded as "strangers" who could alternatively be welcomed hospitably or enslaved or put to death. What mores existed were based on unreflective customs that seemed to have been inherited from time immemorial. What we call *morality* began as the rules or commandments of a deity or various deities, in that moral beliefs required some kind of supernatural or mystical reinforcement or sanctification to be accepted by a community. Only later, beginning with the ancient Greeks, did *ethics* emerge, based on rational discourse and reflection. The shift from blind custom to a commanding morality and finally to a rational ethics occurred with the rise of cities and urban cosmopolitanism, although by no means did custom and morality diminish in importance. Humanity, gradually disengaging its social organisation from the biological facts of blood ties, began to admit the "stranger" and increasingly recognise itself as a shared community of human beings (and ultimately a community of citizens) rather than an ethnic folk or group of kinsmen.

In this primordial and socially formative world, other human biological traits were also reworked from the strictly natural to the social. One of these was the fact of age and its distinctions. In social groups among early humans, the absence of a written language helped to confer on the elderly a high degree of status, for it was they who possessed the traditional wisdom of the community, including knowledge of the traditional kinship lines that prescribed marital ties in obedience to extensive incest taboos as well as survival techniques that had to be acquired by both the young and the mature members of the group. In addition, the *biological* fact of gender distinctions was slowly reworked along *social* lines into what were initially complementary sororal and fraternal groups. Women formed their own food-gathering and care-taking groups with their own customs, belief systems, and values, while men formed their own hunting and warrior groups with their own behavioral characteristics, mores, and ideologies.

From everything we know about the socialisation of the biological facts of kinship, age, and gender groups – their elaboration into early institutions – there is no reason to doubt that these groups existed initially in complementary relationships with one another. Each, in effect, needed the others to form a relatively stable whole. No one group "dominated" the others or tried to privilege itself in the normal course of things. Yet even as the biological underpinnings of consociation were, over time, further reworked into social institutions, so the social institutions were slowly reworked, at various periods and in various degrees, into hierarchical structures based on command and obedience. I speak here of a historical trend, in no way predetermined by any mystical force or deity, and one that was often a very limited development among many preliterate or aboriginal cultures and even in certain fairly elaborate civilisations.

Hierarchy in its earliest forms was probably not marked by the harsh qualities it has acquired over history. Elders, at the very beginnings of gerontocracy, were not only respected for their wisdom but were often beloved of the young, with affection that was often reciprocated in kind. We can probably account for the increasing harshness of later gerontocracies by supposing that the elderly, burdened by their failing physical powers and dependent upon their community's goodwill, were more vulnerable to abandonment in periods of material want than any other part of the population. "Even in simple food-gathering cultures," observed anthropologist Paul Radin, "individuals above fifty, let us say, apparently arrogate to themselves certain powers and privileges which benefited themselves specifically, and were not necessarily, if at all, dictated by considerations either of the rights of others or the welfare of the community." In any case, that gerontocracy was probably the earliest form of hierarchy is corroborated by its existence in communities as disparate as the Australian Aborigines, tribal societies in East Africa, and Native communities in the Americas. Many tribal councils throughout the world were really councils of elders, an institution that never completely disappeared (as the word *alderman* suggests), even after they were overlaid by warrior societies, chiefdoms, and kingships.

Patricentricity, in which masculine values, institutions, and forms of behavior prevail over feminine ones, seems to have developed in the wake of gerontocracy. Initially, the emergence of patricentricity may have been a useful adjunct to a life deeply rooted in the primordial natural world; preliterate and early aboriginal societies were essentially small domestic communities in which the authentic centre of material life was the home, not the "men's house" so widely present in later, more elaborate tribal societies. Male rule, if such it can strictly be called, takes on its harshest and most coercive form in *patriarchy*, an institution in which the eldest male of an extended family or clan has a life-and-death command over all other members of the group. Women may be ordered whom to marry, but they are by no means the exclusive or even the principal object of a patriarch's domination. Sons, like daughters, may be ordered how to behave at the patriarch's command or be killed at his whim.

So far as patricentricity is concerned, however, the authority and prerogative of the male are the product of a long, often subtly negotiated development in which the male fraternity edges out the female sorority by virtue of the former's growing "civil" responsibilities. Increasing population, marauding bands of outsiders whose migrations may be induced by drought or other unfavorable conditions, and vendettas of one kind or another, to cite common causes of hostility or war, create a new "civil" sphere side by side with woman's domestic sphere, and the former gradually encroaches upon the latter. With the appearance of cattle-drawn plow agriculture, the male, who is the "master of the beasts," begins to invade the horticultural sphere of woman, whose primacy as the food cultivator and food gatherer gives her cultural preeminence in the community's internal life, slowly diluting her preeminence. Warrior societies and chiefdoms carry the momentum of male dominance to the level of a new material and cultural dispensation. Male dominance becomes extremely active and ultimately yields a world in which male elites dominate not only women but also, in the form of classes, other men. The causes of the emergence of hierarchy are transparent enough: the infirmities of age, increasing population numbers, natural disasters, technological changes that privileged activities of hunting and animal husbandry over horticultural responsibilities, the growth of civil society, and the spread of warfare, all served to enhance the male's standing at the expense of the female's. It must be emphasised that hierarchical domination, however coercive it may be, is not the same thing as class exploitation. As I wrote in *The Ecology of Freedom*,

> Hierarchy must be viewed as institutionalised relationships, relationships that living beings literally institute or create but which are neither ruthlessly fixed by instinct on the one hand nor idiosyncratic on the other. By this, I mean that they must comprise a clearly social structure of coercive and privileged ranks that exist apart from the idiosyncratic individuals who seem to be dominant within a given community, a hierarchy that is guided by a social logic that goes beyond individual interactions or inborn patterns of behavior.

Marxist theorists tend to single out technological advances and the presumed material surpluses they produce to explain the emergence of elite strata – indeed, of exploiting ruling classes; however, this does not tell us why many societies whose environments were abundantly rich in food never produced such strata. That surpluses are necessary to support elites and classes is obvious, as Aristotle pointed out more than two millennia ago, but too many communities that had such resources at their disposal remained quite egalitarian and never "advanced" to hierarchical or class societies.

It is worth emphasising that hierarchical domination, however coercive it may be, is not to be confused with class exploitation. Often the role of high-status individuals is very well-meaning, as in the case of commands given by caring parents to their children, of concerned husbands and wives to each other, or of elderly people to younger ones. In tribal societies, even where a considerable measure of authority accrues to a chief – and most chiefs are advisers rather than rulers – he usually must earn the esteem of the community by interacting with the people, and he can easily be ignored or removed from his position by them. Many chiefs earn their prestige, so essential to their authority, by disposing of gifts, and even by a considerable disaccumulation of their personal goods. The respect accorded to many chiefs is earned, not by hoarding surpluses as a means to power but by disposing of them as evidence of generosity.

By contrast, classes tend to operate along different lines. In class societies power is usually gained by the *acquisition* of wealth, not by its disposal; rulership is guaranteed by outright physical coercion, not simply by persuasion; and the state is the ultimate guarantor of authority. That hierarchy is historically more entrenched than class can perhaps be verified by the fact that, despite sweeping changes in class societies, even of an economically egalitarian kind, women have still been dominated beings for millennia. By the same token, the abolition of class rule and economic exploitation offers no guarantee whatever that elaborate hierarchies and systems of domination will also disappear.

In nonhierarchical societies, certain customs guide human behavior along basically decent lines. Of primary importance among early customs was the principle of the *irreducible minimum* (to use Paul Radin's expression), the shared notion that all members of the same community are entitled to the means of life, irrespective of the amount of work they perform. To deny anyone food, shelter, and the basic means of life because of their infirmities or even their frivolous behavior would have been seen as a heinous denial of the very right to live. Nor were the basic resources needed to sustain the community ever permitted to be privately owned; overriding individualistic control was the broader principle of *usufruct* – the notion that the means of life that were not being used by one group could be used, as needed, by another. Thus, unused land, orchards, and even tools and weapons, if left idle, were often at the disposition of anyone in the community who needed them. Lastly, custom fostered the practice of *mutual aid*, the rather sensible cooperative sharing of things and labour, so that an individual or family in straitened circumstances could expect to be helped by others. Taken as whole, these customs became so sedimented into organic society that they persisted long after hierarchy became oppressive and class society became predominant.

## THE IDEA OF DOMINATING NATURE

Nature, in the sense of the biotic environment from which humans take the simple things they need for survival, often has no meaning to preliterate peoples as a general concept. Immersed in it as they are, even celebrating animistic rituals in an environment they view as a nexus of life, often imputing their own social institutions to the behavior of nonhuman species, as in the case of beaver "lodges" and humanlike spirits, the concept of "nature" as such eludes them. Words that express our conventional notions of nature are not easy to find, if they exist at all, in the languages of aboriginal peoples.

With the rise of hierarchy and domination, however, the seeds were planted for the belief that first nature not only exists as a world that is increasingly distinguishable from the community but one that is hierarchically organised and can be dominated by human beings. The worldview of magic reveals this shift clearly. Here nature was not conceived as a world apart; rather, a practitioner of magic essentially pleaded with the "chief spirit" of a game animal (itself a puzzling figure in the dream world) to coax it in the direction of an arrow or a spear. Later, magic became almost entirely instrumental; the hunter used magical techniques to "coerce" the game to become prey. While the earliest forms of magic may be regarded as the practices of a generally nonhierarchical and egalitarian community, the later kinds of animistic beliefs betray a more or less hierarchical view of the natural world and of latent human powers of domination over reality.

We must emphasise here that the *idea* of dominating nature has its primary source in the domination of human by human and in the structuring of the natural world into a hierarchical chain of being (a static conception, incidentally, that has no relationship to the dynamic evolution of life into increasingly advanced forms of subjectivity and flexibility). The biblical injunction that gave command of the living world to Adam and Noah was above all an expression of a social dispensation. Its idea of dominating nature – so essential to the view of the nonhuman world as an object of domination – can be overcome only through the creation of a society without those class and hierarchical structures that make for rule and obedience in private as well as public life, and the objectifications of reality as mere materials for exploitation. That this revolutionary dispensation would involve changes in attitudes and values should go without saying. But new ecological attitudes and values will remain vaporous if they are not given substance and solidity through real and objective institutions (the structures by which humans concretely interact with each other) and through the tangible realities of everyday life from childrearing to work and play. Until human beings cease to live in societies that are structured around hierarchies as well as economic classes, we shall never be free of domination, however much we may try to dispel it with rituals, incantations, ecotheologies, and the adoption of seemingly "natural" lifeways.

The idea of dominating nature has a history that is almost as old as that of hierarchy itself. Already in the *Gilgamesh* epic of Mesopotamia, a drama whose written form dates back some four thousand years, the hero defies the deities and cuts down their sacred trees in his quest for immortality. The Odyssey is a vast travelogue of the Greek warrior, more canny than heroic, who in his wanderings essentially subdues the nature deities that the Hellenic world had inherited from its less well-known precursors (ironically, the dark pre-Olympian world that has been revived by purveyors of eco-mysticism and spiritualism). Long before the emergence of modern science, "linear" rationality, and "industrial society" (to cite causal factors that are often invoked flippantly by some in the modern ecology movement), hierarchical and class societies laid waste to much of the Mediterranean basin as well as the hillsides of China, beginning a vast remaking and often despoliation of the planet.

To be sure, human second nature, in inflicting harm on first nature, created no Garden of Eden. More often than not, it despoiled much that was beautiful, creative, and dynamic in the biotic world, just as it ravaged human life itself in murderous warfare, genocide, and acts of heartless oppression. Social ecology maintains that the future of human life goes hand in hand with the future of the nonhuman world, yet it does not overlook the fact that the harm that hierarchical and class society inflicted on the natural world was more than matched by the harm it inflicted on much of humanity.

However troubling the ills produced by second nature, the customs of the irreducible minimum, usufruct, and mutual aid cannot be ignored in any account of anthropology and history. These customs persisted well into historical times and surfaced sometimes explosively in massive popular uprisings, from revolts in ancient Sumer to the present time. Many of those revolts demanded the recovery of caring and communistic values, at times when these were coming under the onslaught of elitist and class oppression. Indeed, despite the armies that roamed the landscape of warring areas, the tax-gatherers who plundered ordinary village peoples, and the daily abuses that overseers inflicted on peasants and workers, community life still persisted and retained many of the cherished values of a more egalitarian past. Neither ancient despots nor feudal lords could fully obliterate them in peasant villages and in the towns with independent craft associations. In ancient Greece, a rational philosophy that rejected the encumbering of thought and political life by extravagant wants, as well as a religion based on austerity, tended to scale down needs and delimit human appetites for material goods. Together they served to slow the pace of technological innovation sufficiently such that when new means of production were developed, they could be sensitively integrated into a balanced society. In medieval times, markets were still modest, usually local affairs, in which guilds exercised strict control over prices, competition, and the quality of the goods produced by their members.

## "GROW OR DIE"

But just as hierarchies and class structures had acquired momentum and permeated much of society, so too the market began to acquire a life of its own and extended its reach beyond a few limited regions into the depths of vast continents. Where exchange had once been primarily a means to provide for essential needs, limited by guilds or by moral and religious restrictions, long-distance trade subverted those limits. Not only did trade place a high premium on techniques for increasing production, it also became the progenitor of new needs, many of them wholly artificial, and gave a tremendous impetus to consumption and the growth of capital. First in northern Italy and the European lowlands, and later – and most decisively – in England during the seventeenth and eighteenth centuries, the production of goods exclusively for sale and profit (the production of the capitalistic commodity) rapidly swept aside all cultural and social barriers to market growth.

By the late-eighteenth and early-nineteenth centuries, the new industrial capitalist class, with its factory system and commitment to limitless expansion, had embarked on its colonisation of the entire world, including most aspects of personal life. Unlike the feudal nobility, with its cherished lands and castles, the bourgeoisie had no home but the marketplace and its bank vaults. As a class, it turned more and more of the world into a domain of factories. In the ancient and medieval worlds, entrepreneurs had normally invested profits in land and lived like country gentry, given the prejudices of the times against "ill-gotten" gains from trade. But the industrial capitalists of the modern world spawned a bitterly competitive marketplace that placed a high premium on industrial expansion and the commercial power it conferred, functioning as though growth were an end in itself.

In social ecology it is crucially important to recognise that industrial growth did not and does not result from changes in cultural outlook alone – least of all from the impact of scientific and technological rationality on society. Growth occurs above all from *harshly objective factors* churned up by the expansion of the market itself, *factors that are largely impervious to moral considerations and efforts at ethical persuasion.* Indeed, despite the close association between capitalist development and technological innovation, the most driving imperative of any enterprise in the harshly capitalist marketplace, given the savagely dehumanising competition that prevails there, is the need of an enterprise to grow in order to avoid perishing at the hands of its savage rivals. Important as even greed may be as a motivating force, sheer survival requires that the entrepreneur must expand his or her productive apparatus in order to remain ahead of others. Each capitalist, in short, must try to devour his or her rivals – or else be devoured by them. The key to this law of life – to survival – is expansion, and the quest for ever-greater profits, to be invested, in turn, in still further expansion. Indeed, the notion of progress, once regarded as faith in the evolution of greater human cooperation and care, is now identified with ever greater competition and reckless economic growth.

The effort by many well-intentioned ecology theorists and their admirers to reduce the ecological crisis to a cultural crisis rather than a social one becomes very obfuscatory and misleading. However ecologically well-meaning an entrepreneur may be, the harsh fact is that his or her very survival in the marketplace precludes the development of a meaningful ecological orientation. The adoption of ecologically sound practices places a morally concerned entrepreneur at a striking and indeed fatal disadvantage in a competitive relationship with a rival – who, operating without ecological guidelines and moral constraints, produces cheap commodities at lower costs and reaps higher profits for further capital expansion. The marketplace has its own law of survival: only the most unscrupulous can rise to the top of that competitive struggle.

Indeed, to the extent that environmental movements and ideologies merely moralise about the wickedness of our anti-ecological society and call for changes in personal lifestyles and attitudes, they obscure the need for concerted social action and tend to deflect the struggle for far-reaching social change. Meanwhile, corporations are skillfully manipulating this popular desire for personal ecologically sound practices by cultivating ecological mirages. So it is that we see, among hundreds of similar advertisements, Mercedes-Benz declaim, in a two-page magazine advertisement, decorated with a bison painting from a Paleolithic cave wall, that "We must work to make progress more environmentally sustainable by including environmental themes in the planning of new products." If such messages are commonplace in Germany, one of western Europe's worst polluters, the same advertising is equally manipulative in the United States, where leading polluters piously declare that for them, "Every Day is Earth Day."

The point social ecology emphasises is not that moral and spiritual persuasion and renewal are meaningless or unnecessary; they are necessary and can be educational. But modern capitalism is *structurally* amoral and hence impervious to moral appeals. The modern marketplace is driven by imperatives of its own, irrespective of what kind of CEO sits in a corporation's driver's seat or holds on to its handlebars. The direction it follows depends not upon ethical prescriptions and personal inclinations but upon objective laws of profit or loss, growth or death, eat or be eaten, and the like. The maxim "Business is business" explicitly tells us that ethical, religious, psychological, and emotional factors have virtually no place in the predatory world of production, profit, and growth. It is grossly misleading to think that we can divest this harsh, indeed mechanistic world of its objective characteristics by means of ethical appeals.

A society based on the law of "grow or die" as its all-pervasive imperative must of necessity have a devastating impact on first nature. Nor does "growth" here refer to population growth; the current wisdom of population-boomers to the contrary, the most serious disruptors of ecological cycles are found in the large industrial centres of the world, which are not only poisoning water and air but producing the greenhouse gases that are melting the ice caps and threatening to flood vast areas of the planet. Suppose we could somehow cut the world's population in half: would growth and the despoliation of the earth be reduced at all? Capital would insist that it was "indispensable" to own two or three of every appliance, motor vehicle, or electronic gadget, where one would more than suffice if not be too many. In addition, the military would continue to demand ever more lethal instruments of death and devastation, of which new models would be provided annually.

Nor would "softer" technologies, if produced by a grow-or-die market, fail to be used for destructive capitalistic ends. Two centuries ago, large forested areas in England were hacked into fuel for iron forges with axes that had not changed appreciably since the Bronze Age, and ordinary sails guided ships laden with commodities to all parts of the world well into the nineteenth century. Indeed, much of the United States was cleared of its forests, wildlife, and its Indigenous inhabitants with tools and weapons that could have easily been recognised, however much they were modified, by Renaissance people centuries earlier. What modern technics did was accelerate a process that had been well under way at the close of the Middle Ages. It cannot be held solely responsible for endeavors that were under way for centuries; it essentially abetted damage caused by the ever-expanding market system, whose roots, in turn, lay in one of history's most fundamental social transformations: the elaboration of a system of production and distribution based on exchange rather than complementarity and mutual aid.

## AN ECOLOGICAL SOCIETY

Social ecology is an appeal not only for moral regeneration but, and above all, for social reconstruction along ecological lines. It emphasises that, taken by itself, an ethical appeal to the powers that be, based on blind market forces and ruthless competition, is certain to be futile. Indeed, taken by itself, such an appeal obscures the real power relationships that prevail today by making the attainment of an ecological society seem merely a matter of changing individual attitudes, spiritual renewal, or quasi-religious redemption.

Although always mindful of the importance of a new ethical outlook, social ecology seeks to redress the ecological abuses that the prevailing society has inflicted on the natural world by going to the structural as well as the subjective sources of notions like the domination of first nature. That is, it challenges the entire system of domination itself – its economy, its misuse of technics, its administrative apparatus, its degradations of political life, its destruction of the city as a centre of cultural development, indeed the entire panoply of its moral hypocrisies and defiling of the human spirit – and seeks to eliminate the hierarchical and class edifices that have imposed themselves on humanity and defined the relationship between nonhuman and human nature. It advances an ethics of complementarity in which human beings play a supportive role in perpetuating the integrity of the biosphere – the potentiality of human beings to be the most conscious products of natural evolution. Indeed, humans have an ethical responsibility to function creatively in the unfolding of that evolution. Social ecology thus stresses the need to embody its ethics of complementarity in palpable social institutions that will make human beings conscious ethical agents in promoting the well-being of themselves and the nonhuman world. It seeks the enrichment of the evolutionary process by the diversification of life-forms and the application of reason to a wondrous remaking of the planet along ecological lines. Notwithstanding most romantic views, "Mother Nature" does not necessarily "know best." To oppose activities of the corporate world does not require one to become naïvely biocentric. Indeed by the same token, to applaud humanity's potential for foresight, rationality, and technological achievement does not make one anthropocentric. The loose usage of such buzzwords must be brought to a definitive end by reflective discussion, not by deprecating denunciations.

Social ecology, in effect, recognises that – like it or not – the future of life on this planet pivots on the future of society. It contends that evolution, both in first nature and in second, is not yet complete. Nor are the two realms so separated from each other that we must choose one or the other – either natural evolution, with its "biocentric" halo, or social evolution, as we have known it up to now, with its "anthropocentric" halo – as the basis for a creative biosphere. We must go beyond both the natural and the

# LET'S MAKE
# SOLIDARITY REAL!

**SUPPORT DOPE MAGAZINE**

# BUY US A PINT?

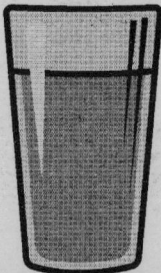

## FOR THE PRICE OF
## A PINT PER MONTH (£5)

**YOU CAN** = 50 DOPE MAGAZINE
**MAKE**
**POSSIBLE** = £150 FOR A VENDOR

YOUR MONTHLY FIVER MEANS £1800 A YEAR FOR THOSE
WHO NEED IT MOST

## LET'S MAKE SOLIDARITY REAL!

SUPPORT DOPE MAGAZINE

To donate:
patreon.com/dopemag

social toward a new synthesis that contains the best of both. Such a synthesis must transcend both first and second nature in the form of a creative, self-conscious, and therefore "free nature," in which human beings intervene in natural evolution with their best capacities – their ethical sense, their unequaled capacity for conceptual thought, and their remarkable powers and range of communication.

But such a goal remains mere rhetoric unless a *movement* gives it logistical and social tangibility. How are we to organise such a movement? Logistically, "free nature" is unattainable without the decentralisation of cities into confederally united communities sensitively tailored to the natural areas in which they are located. Ecotechnologies, solar, wind, methane, and other renewable sources of energy; organic forms of agriculture; and the design of humanly scaled, versatile industrial installations to meet the regional needs of confederated municipalities – all must be brought into the service of an ecologically sound world based on an ethics of complementarity. It means too an emphasis not only on recycling but on the production of high-quality goods that can, in many cases, last for generations. It means the replacement of needlessly insensate labour with creative work and an emphasis on artful craftspersonship in preference to mechanised production. It means the free time to be artful and to fully engage in public affairs. One would hope that the sheer availability of goods, the mechanisation of production, and the freedom to choose one's material lifestyle would sooner or later influence people to practice moderation in all aspects of life as a response to the consumerism promoted by the capitalist market.

But no ethics or vision of an ecological society, however inspired, can be meaningful unless it is embodied in a living politics. By *politics*, I do not mean the statecraft practiced by what we call politicians – namely, representatives elected or selected to manage public affairs and formulate policies as guidelines for social life. To social ecology, politics means what it meant in the democratic *polis* of classical Athens some two thousand years ago: direct democracy, the formulation of policies by directly democratic popular assemblies, and the administration of those policies by mandated coordinators who can easily be recalled if they fail to abide by the decision of the assembly's citizens. I am very mindful that Athenian politics, even in its most democratic periods, was marred by the existence of slavery and patriarchy, and by the exclusion of the stranger from public life. In this respect, to be sure, it differed very little from most of the other ancient Mediterranean civilisations – and certainly ancient Asian ones – of the time. What made Athenian politics unique, however, was that it produced institutions that were extraordinarily democratic – even directly so – by comparison with the republican institutions of the so-called "democracies" of today's world. Either directly or indirectly, the Athenian democracy inspired later, more all-encompassing direct democracies, such as many medieval European towns, the little-known Parisian "sections" (or neighborhood assemblies) of 1793 that propelled the French Revolution in a highly radical direction, and more indirectly,

New England town meetings and other, more recent attempts at civic self-governance.

Any self-managed community, however, that tries to live in isolation and develop self-sufficiency risks the danger of becoming parochial, even racist. Hence the need to extend the ecological politics of a direct democracy into confederations of ecocommunities, and to foster a healthy interdependence, rather than an introverted, stultifying independence. Social ecology would be obliged to embody its ethics in a politics of libertarian municipalism, in which municipalities conjointly gain rights to self-governance through networks of confederal councils, to which towns and cities would be expected to send their mandated, recallable delegates to adjust differences. All decisions would have to be ratified by a majority of the popular assemblies of the confederated towns and cities. This institutional process could be initiated in the neighbourhoods of giant cities as well as in networks of small towns. In fact, the formation of numerous "town halls" has already repeatedly been proposed in cities as large as New York and Paris, only to be defeated by well-organised elitist groups that sought to centralise power rather than allow its decentralisation.

Power will always belong to elite and commanding strata if it is not institutionalised in face-to-face democracies, among people who are fully empowered as social beings to make decisions in new communal assemblies. Attempts to empower people in this manner and form constitute an abiding challenge to the nation-state – that is, a dual power in which the free municipality exists in open tension with the nation-state. Power that does not belong to the people invariably belongs to the state and the exploitative interests it represents. Which is not to say that diversity is not a desideratum; to the contrary, it is the source of cultural creativity. Still it never should be celebrated in a nationalistic sense of "apartness" from the general interests of humanity as a whole, or else it will regress into the parochialism of folkdom and tribalism.

Should the full reality of citizenship in all its discursiveness and political vitality begin to wane, its disappearance would mark an unprecedented loss in human development. Citizenship, in the classical sense of the term, which involved a lifelong, ethically oriented education in the art of participation in public affairs (not the empty form of national legitimation that it so often consists of today), would disappear. Its loss would mean the atrophying of a communal life beyond the limits of the family, the waning of a civic sensibility to the point of the shriveled ego, the complete replacement of the public arena with the private world and with private pursuits.

The failure of a rational, socially committed ecology movement would yield a mechanised, aesthetically arid, and administered society, composed of vacuous egos at best and totalitarian automata at worst. Before the planet was rendered physically uninhabitable, there would be few humans who would be able to inhabit it.

Alternatively, a truly ecological society would open the vista of a "free nature" with a sophisticated eco-technology based on solar, wind, and water; carefully treated fossil fuels would be sited to produce power to meet rationally conceived needs. Production would occur entirely for use, not for profit, and the distribution of goods would occur entirely to meet human needs based on norms established by citizens' assemblies and confederations of assemblies. Decisions by the community would be made according to direct, face-to-face procedures with all the coordinative judgments by mandated delegates. These judgments, in turn, would be referred back for discussion, approval, modification, or rejection by the assembly of assemblies (or Commune of communes) as a whole, reflecting the wishes of the fully assembled majority.

We cannot tell how much technology will be expanded a few decades from now, let alone a few generations. The growth and the prospects it is likely to open over the course of this century alone are too dazzling even for the most imaginative utopian to envision. If nothing else, we have been swept into a permanent technological and communications revolution whose culmination it is impossible to foresee. This amassing of power and knowledge opens two radically opposing prospects: either humanity will truly destroy itself and its habitat, or it will create a garden, a fruitful and benign world that not even the most fanciful utopian, Charles Fourier, could have imagined.

It is fitting that such dire alternatives should appear now and in such extreme forms. Unless social ecology – with its naturalistic outlook, its developmental interpretations of natural and social phenomena, its emphasis on discipline with freedom and responsibility with imagination – can be brought to the service of such historic ends, humanity may well prove to be incapable of changing the world. We cannot defer the need to deal with these prospects indefinitely: either a movement will arise that will bestir humanity into action, or the last great chance in history for the complete emancipation of humanity will perish in unrestrained self-destruction.

————————

**Murray Bookchin** (1921-2006) was a major figure in anarchist and utopian political theory for six decades. The author of more than two dozen books, he wrote extensively on technology, urbanism, ecology, history, and philosophy, and was the cofounder and director emeritus of the Institute for Social Ecology. His many books include *Post-Scarcity Anarchism*, *Toward an Ecological Society*, *The Ecology of Freedom*, *From Urbanization to Cities* and the four-volume history *The Third Revolution: Popular Movements in the Revolutionary Era*. This essay was originally published in 1986 in *The Modern Crisis*. It was subsequently revised by Bookchin and then updated in 2022, as it appears here.

# REBER APO IS A PERMACULTURALIST

## PERMACULTURE AND POLITICAL TRANSFORMATION IN NORTH EAST SYRIA

### Viyan Qerecox

---

I f Reber Apo, the imprisoned leader of the Kurdish liberation movement, was a gardener, I would expect his garden to be colourful and wild, spilling out beyond its borders, a glorious mixture of vegetables, trees, flowers and vines. Drawing on his writings on political transformation, I imagine him to be a permaculturalist, creating gardens based on the wisdom of nature.

Permaculture is a design system that strives to make ecological spaces sustainable and productive. But the approach is also geared towards other kinds of design, whether it's architecture, urban planning, organisational structures or even political systems. The word comes from a combination of "permanent" and "culture," so at its most fundamental it's an attempt to develop a culture of permanence. In this case, permanent does not mean static –

like nature, the system must grow and develop as it responds to internal and external change – but it is permanent in that it is not geared towards self-destruction in the way that our current agricultural systems tend to be.

Permaculture takes a values-centred approach, so the ethics of "earth care, people care and fair shares" hold the centre, and from there productive and sustainable outputs shape the form. Permaculture is a holistic system: it insists that we look not just at component parts of a design, but at the relationships between them, and how they come together to create a whole. A permaculture garden aims to take inspiration from the way in which ecological systems sustain themselves in nature, with the saying "think like a forest, act like a meadow" giving a poetic insight into the permaculture approach.

Forests and meadows are both ecosystems that sustain an astounding diversity of life within a "closed loop" resilient system. They don't require external fertiliser, chemical pesticides or artificial watering systems. And yet they sustain impressive numbers of plant and animal species, as well as countless fungi, bacteria and micro-organisms in the soil, which are also crucial to keeping the system healthy. A permaculture garden would seek to replicate these patterns and relationships. Rather than growing plants in isolated rows, a permaculture garden would group plants together so they can work collectively. A classic example of this – drawn from indigenous knowledge – is the 'three sisters' planting pattern. Maize, climbing beans and squash are grown together, so that the squash covers the soil to keep moisture in the ground; the climbing beans put nutrients into the soil that the other plants need; and the maize provides a climbing structure for the beans. If planted in this way, this vegetable patch preserves soil quality, reduces need for water and improves harvest yield – so it's sustainable and efficient. This is one of many approaches that permaculture harnesses through its twelve principles, which encompass concepts such as "produce no waste," "use and value diversity," "creatively use and respond to change," and "design from pattern to detail."

Making the leap from gardens to revolutionary approaches in political organising, we can see a lot of useful parallels that show us how to build movements, organisations and communities that are productive, sustainable and holistic. But before we explore the compatibilities of permaculture and political transformation, let's look at why it even makes sense to do it.

One reason has already been mentioned: permaculture takes a holistic approach to developing strategies and solutions, and having a coherent framework is crucial to having an effective political strategy. This is a strength of the Kurdish liberation ideology as shaped by Reber Apo and, more recently, the New Paradigm. It already takes a holistic ideological approach, recognising the interconnection between patriarchy, capitalism, the state and ecological destruction. In the West, too often we fire-fight between issues, not developing or expressing a coherent ideology that effectively highlights and challenges the structural causes of what we are fighting against.

Permaculture is also a useful tool for developing a new way of doing politics – one that is less shaped by the relations of domination that have characterised politics since the rise of the state. Patriarchy and capitalism enact dominating relations between people, while at the same time establishing a dominating relationship with the environment. So, the way that we relate to each other is inextricable from how we relate to nature, but we can look to nature for a different approach. A new way of doing politics means rejecting hierarchical and patriarchal approaches and, instead, embraces an ecology – and permaculture can shed some light on what an ecological way of doing politics could look like. The political transformation that has been happening through the Rojava Revolution in North East Syria recognises the importance of this shift in mentality, which is why it is particularly interesting to analyse the movement through the lens of permaculture.

One principle of permaculture that invites interesting analyses is "creatively use and respond to change," which is sometimes conceptualised as "the problem is the solution." – sometimes, when things aren't going as they should, the solution lies within the problem. The most famous example is that if your garden is overrun by slugs, rather than investing in chemical pesticides or spending hours plucking slugs from lettuce leaves, you could introduce some ducks into your garden. The ducks will happily munch on the slugs while also producing delicious eggs and healthy fertiliser for your garden.

Politically, "creatively use and respond to change" can mean anything from repurposing viral right-wing slogans and brands with our own message ("Make Rojava Green Again" can be an example of this) to using the chaos and collapse of current political and economic systems as an opportunity to organise and build resistance. It's also about being able to see things in unconventional ways. An interesting example of this is the New Paradigm of the Kurdish liberation movement. For a long time, the answer to the "Kurdish Problem" was assumed to be a Kurdish state. But through the New paradigm, the problem itself becomes the solution – statelessness is the answer to how to build a truly liberated political system.

Permaculture also teaches us to "use and value the margins and edges" and "use and value diversity." In the garden, this means using polyculture growing techniques, like the 'three sisters' planting pattern described above. It acknowledges that monoculture – just having one kind of plant – does not exist in nature, or is a symptom of a system out of balance. Furthermore, we can observe that the spaces between systems – the 'margins and edges' – are areas of high diversity and productivity. This includes spaces like tidal pools or riverbanks, where unique forms of life develop and flourish. These principles are relevant to political organising in lots of ways that are encompassed by democratic confederalism.

Democratic modernity embraces diversity and plurality, rejecting the hegemonic and fascist tendencies of capitalist modernity and the state system. In politics, we embrace the edges through organising as and alongside marginalised communities. The Kurdish liberation movement also teaches us to not focus all of our energy on the centre of power – the state and corporations – but to also build power around the edges, in society and in the places where the state does not have a monopoly on power. This way you're able to grow revolution on fertile ground, with many voices feeding into the process and embracing the diversity that will give a revolutionary system sustainability.

A truly sustainable system is able to absorb and work with change, staying true to the values at the heart of the system while adjusting the methods. The permaculture principle that describes this approach is "apply self-regulation and accept feedback." Simply put, this means don't take more than what you need, be aware of the impacts of your actions on the world around you, and continuously readjust your approach to ensure that you are aligned with the values at the core of your work. It doesn't take much effort to see how this applies to ecology and politics equally.

This concept is encompassed by the Zapatista approach of "walking, we ask questions," which encapsulates how revolution is an ongoing process that requires constant reflection, questioning and readjusting our path. Tekmil, the Kurdish liberation movement's practice of criticism and self-criticism, is also crucial in this process. Through giving criticism and evaluating our work, we ensure that we stay on track, and are being as effective as possible. Examples of this include recent actions of the Autonomous Administration in adjusting the role of Tev Dem to support the neighbourhood communes to work in a genuinely democratic way, as well as changes from the Economy Committee to strengthen the collective nature of cooperatives, rather than acting too much like private initiatives.

By dismantling the boundary between the political and ecological realms, we can strengthen our ability to build movements that are resilient, dynamic and effective. Democratic confederalism and the Kurdish liberation movement have a natural affinity to ecological thinking, so it's no surprise that the new paradigm places ecological sustainability as one of the three core pillars of a revolutionary approach. As the ecological values at the heart of the revolution are applied to the reality in North East Syria, permaculture can be a useful tool to frame the environmental approach. Conversely, Western political movements struggle to meaningfully integrate sustainability into broader political movements, and ecological campaigns often take a highly technical and state-centred approach. Through weaving a permaculture approach into our political organising, we can develop a more holistic and coherent politics. We can nurture a revolution that is built on mutuality and diversity, that enables us to live freely with each other and with nature.

---

**Viyan Qerecox** (Natalia Szarek) has been involved in radical struggles for social change in the UK for over 15 years, particularly in ecological, food sovereignty and feminist movements and struggles for community power. In 2019 she spent a year as an internationalist volunteer in Rojava and has continued to work with the Kurdistan freedom movement since returning to the UK.

For more information on permaculture, see:

**labofii.net/docs/13attitudes.pdf**

**permacultureprinciples.com**

# ECOLOGICAL CATASTROPHE

## NATURE TALKS BACK

### Pelşîn Tolhildan

---

Would a human being set fire to their own house? Yes, they would! Would a human cut the branch of a tree they sit on? Yes, indeed! Would humanity, as often repeated in Yasar Kemal's novel Ince Memed, pull a knife on the table they eat on? Oh yes! Would a human being grow up to call the mother womb that gave birth to them "savage"? Definitely!

Until that fire comes to surround them, until that branch falls on their head, until that knife touches their bone, until that nest completely closes to them so that they are left breathless, human beings would, have done, and unfortunately still continue to do all of the aforementioned things. Of course, not all of a sudden, but ever since they became victims of human-made mentalities and systems. We can call it the "ecology issue" or we can call it nature teaching us a lesson – in any case, we are paying the price for our betrayal of nature.

Every phenomenon whose value we do not appreciate makes us pay the price. The bigger the value we do not recognise, the bigger the price we pay for betraying it. If it is our own nature whose value we do not appreciate, the nature into which we are born, the price will be a global warming that burns us. It will become a forest fire and roast us; it will become a flood and drown us; it will turn into ice and freeze us; it will become contamination and poison us. And for every day that we ignore nature's calls to solve the problem, death will hit us even harder.

But has it always been the case that we did not recognise the importance of nature? Is this how we developed? How could we become the enemies and killers of the oceans, forests, lands, and air that have given birth to us? And how could the same nature, which is our birth nest, turn into fire raining down on us, into flood, and into poison that throws up on us? These are now questions that no human who lives on this world can escape any longer. Understanding where, when and how this harm began must be the responsibility of every human who wants to live in freedom. So, in order to understand the issue, let's start at the roots. Let us have a look at what kind of mentality we have lost and how it related to nature:

"Natural society's mental world relies on an animated understanding of nature. It believes that every phenomenon in nature has a spirit. Spirits are understood as features that secure aliveness. In the totemic religions the concept of an external, ruling deity apart from the self is not yet developed. Great effort is made to be in harmony with nature's spirits. Failure to do so is similar to death. When this is the fundamental perspective on nature, an extraordinary need for harmony emerges. According to the most fundamental principle of ecology, we are face to face with life. Effort is made to avoid societal life from going against natural forces. When constructing religions and ethics, the most fundamental principle is harmony with the environment and natural forces. This principle is so deeply rooted in the mentality that it is valued as a religious and moral tradition. In fact, this is the principle of life's natural flow manifesting itself in human society. There is no being that does not consider its environment. Short-term deviations are overcome in a stream, within external and internal conditions; otherwise, by being completely left out of the system, they cease to exist. The importance of the principle of ecology for human society derives from this fundamental feature of nature."

In natural society, all members organically participate in the entirety of life. Everyone is a genuine, essential part of society. Belief and perceptions are common. The concepts of lying and cheating have not yet developed. It is as though they speak the same childish language with nature. To dominate nature, to abuse it, is the biggest sin, taboo, and against their ethics and beliefs, their newly developed societal rules. What was turned upside down in statist society is this religious and ethical fundamental principle; humanity has increasingly lost touch with this ethical understanding:

> "The rise of statist society constitutes a fundamental break with this vital principle. The development of the environmental, ecological question along with this particular direction that society has taken is thus fundamentally linked to the beginning of civilization. The civilization of classed society is a society at conflict with nature. The main reason for this phenomenal question has to do with the counter-revolutionary mentality of this new society."[1]

Indeed, the break from natural society and the transition to the statist-paradigm have come at a heavy price. Once the world's ties were loosened and removed, the bonds between nature and social life transformed from a harmonic, mutually nourishing relationship to a subject-object relation. The image of a mother-woman, who feeds a child with one breast and an animal cub with the other breast has become laughable, even fictional to our eyes. In the Western enlightenment tradition, we started to say: there is no difference between the cries of an animal or the grinding of the machine when experimenting.

> **"The most realistic way of looking for the roots of the increasingly deepening ecological crisis, which develops parallel to the crisis of the social system, is to consider the beginning of civilization. The more alienation within society happens due to domination within society, the more the alienation from nature is realised."[2]**

**ABDULLAH ÖCALAN**

The human has become cruel towards nature by oppressing its own species. The same mentality reached horrific dimensions at the hands of the church in the torture of witches (the wise women).

The result of this struggle in the name of conquering irrationality under the banner of reason was complete irrationality in turn – in the name of "obtaining the truth," truth itself was betrayed. After our mentality broke away from natural society's, the name of the societal system changed but its mentality did not. It is a mentality that breaks from natural society, betrays itself and nature, and every day cuts the branch of the tree it sits on. It does not matter whether we call this mentality formation dominant, statist, feudal or capitalist. All of these together constitute a break from natural society and nature. They make up the opposite pole to natural society, in other words, they are anti-nature. They are anti-life, anti-human. Thus, they are anti-ecological.

If sociality and nature managed to live together for thousands of years in harmony, it means that the human, in fact the human of natural society, proved this reality: the human is not the opposite of the same nature it came from, on the contrary, it is nature's very own child. And thus, they can live together without eradicating each other. Contrary to the long imposition of Western mentality, neither is nature savage, nor do humans need to survive by fighting against and conquering this 'savagery.' This is a philosophical lie that tries to break the truth into subject-object dichotomies, incites conflict, and aims to perpetuate the currently hegemonic system as eternal. It is a story that alienates humans and nature from each other – an alienation that has an irreversible structure under capitalism.

Everybody was turned into a subject of this massacre on nature in the name of bravery, in the name of achieving victory in the war against the 'wild.' Now it is the turn of this story's 'object' to speak. Now, it is talking. And every day, it gives us the message that we need to take it seriously. Whether we see it or not, now the world belongs to nature – it cries that it no longer wants to be the object of this story.

Nature has an evolutionary character that has been in action for millions of years. This is not about the fittest exterminating the less fit. Perhaps it is true that the less fit decrease in numbers; however, the smallest organisms to the great ecosystems in nature arrange, adapt and change themselves according to changing conditions. In other words, nature resists. It creates its own mechanisms to defend itself. Human-caused issues upset nature's balance and result in catastrophes that bring about great changes. When humans tried to conquer and dominate nature and to engage in a competition to show nature who is the master, they forgot a fairly simple fact: nature was their home, their birth nest, it was the life atmosphere to which humans owe their bread, water, their very existence, and happiness.

> **"**
>
> **The fundamental reason for ecological problems is the ruling power rendering an anti-natural life possible through its tyranny and lies. By denying nature's role in life and by replacing it with fake deities and creators, it is possible to call nature 'blind force.'[3]**
>
> **"**

**ABDULLAH ÖCALAN**

But the eyes and hearts that were so focused on profit remained oblivious to this naked reality. While the belief was held that nature has been muted after all these attacks, the one forced to their knees was the human in the end. Nature has managed to express itself in many ways, while it is humans who swallow their tongue. In order to see the ways in which we pay the price for destroying the same nature we owe our life to, let us have a brief look at some natural disaster news at the time when this article was first written (2009–2010):

Experts claim that the flood in Pakistan and the extreme heat in Russia are linked to the extraordinary impacts of global warming. Due to flood and landslides, more than 700 people in China, more than 1,600 people in Pakistan, and more than 130 people in India have been killed. Thousands of people, disappeared; millions of people lost their homes. In the smog and dust that covers Moscow and which resulted in drought, toxic material has been discovered. In the fires that have started in more than 600 different areas, 50 people in Russia have been killed. The fires started to affect the military areas so that the explosive materials in these regions were carried to other areas by the authorities. Bush fires rage in south Australia without cease and have so far killed over 200. The forest fires in Greece cannot be brought under control. The fire that started near Athens is approaching the city centre. Due to the spread of the fire, strengthened by the wind, a state of emergency has been declared. Global warming is melting the glaciers of Mount Kilimanjaro, which is considered a world heritage site.

Things have only worsened ever since. More recently, a scientific report by the WWF revealed that 60% of animal populations have been wiped out by humanity since 1970, with disastrous effects on nature and its human children. It seems that ecological catastrophe has advanced to such a degree that it would take up to 7 million years for nature to recover even if destruction was halted immediately. Entire species are predicted to die out, countless hurricanes, droughts, floods, wildfires and glaciers melting are anticipated. Experts speak of a "climate genocide."

The most affected humans of these developments are in the Global South, indigenous and rural communities in particular, whose relationship to nature is symbiotic and organic. The ecological crisis is also caused by the military industrial complex and wars are often triggered by changes in the climate, due to unsustainable capitalist interests in natural resources. Yet states and companies, the main culprits of ecological catastrophe, consciously withdraw from legal and international responsibilities and resort to various means of denying the obvious. As if to summon the end of the world, they announce further destruction of natural habitats, and the exploitation of life.

Is it possible that humans call human-made catastrophes "natural disasters" in order to cover up their own guilt? Or perhaps, by calling these disasters "God's plan," they try to find a divine partner in crime? In reality, no disaster is able to grow this much and claim so many lives without the impact of humans. Indeed, human-made industry, technology, wars, weapons (chemical, biological or any other kind of weaponry) and many other developments or inventions burn nature – and nature burns back. The more it gets destroyed at the hands of humans, the more it brings death to humanity.

These are neither expressions of a pessimistic point of view, nor do they reflect the propaganda of a science fiction hero that is looking for a piece of land to start a new social life with the seeds in their hands after all the lands have been eradicated. Maybe these catastrophes have not touched all of us individually yet. Perhaps we have not yet seen hundreds of people die at once in front of our eyes. But everybody who lives on this planet needs to know that the human-made catastrophes are as close to us as our breath, water and bread, even as the blood running in our veins. This nature is no longer the nature of thousands of years ago. This nature is a nature that has been manipulated. We are under the siege of a nature that has been hurt, divided, defiled, poisoned, harmed and made to bleed.

Through certain observations, humans were previously able to more or less identify and estimate the location, time, extent of such disasters and act accordingly. But nowadays we are not even aware of how exactly we harm nature as humans. Who knows how many nuclear tests there are? How much have our seas, our lands been contaminated by petrol or toxic material? We don't know exactly the amount of greenhouse gases and carbon contamination. Who would know the biodiversity and ecosystems that were eliminated by the hands of soldiers that also burned down the forests of Kurdistan? In short, there is an uncontrolled attack on nature by humans. That is why perhaps nature will strike back with a horrible surprise through a series of uncontrollable disasters that we cannot anticipate. Our aim is neither to demonise humans, nor to advocate for a protection of nature that is separate from the human and society. We merely discuss a factual reality that was designed by human hand, mind and action.

Those concerned with ecological problems are aware that the system that has deepened and further led these issues to unsustainability is capitalism. "Europe's individualism has come to embody the massacre of the society and its ecology. The capitalist system's establishment of its dominance, its move from individuality to individualism, not only reversed social gains, but also caused the biggest ecological deviation in history."[4]

Ecological issues and their sources have been discussed through a variety of philosophical, societal, eco-feminist and many other perspectives and have thus become visible as a serious problem for years now. Perhaps the real problem then is how much this problem is being felt. This concerns the real powers of the society – because when the real forces that make up society start to sense this problem, a large part of the solution will have been achieved.

> "The actual ecological phenomenon is to prevent the relationship between nature and society becoming a gap. If this gap is not closed as soon as possible, the society will turn into dinosaurs."[5]

When we look at the issue from this perspective, we can make a global effort to sense the problem and bring it to the agenda. The World Social Forum's slogan "Another World is Possible," the UN's climate conferences, locally organised free ecological forums, social urban movements, the agreement of powerful countries on issues like reducing carbon intensity, discussions on bio-security, the creation of ecological collectives, hundreds of thousands of activists around the world risking their lives to draw attention to ecological issues, the discussions of eco-socialists and eco-feminists, the organisation of ecology festivals, UNESCO compiling a list on endangered world heritage, sustainable energy conferences, and thousands of actions, events, organisations, work, increasing awareness and activism – are all signs of an effort to close this gap between nature and society. However, when considering the size of the catastrophe we are facing, these initiatives remain dispersed and insufficient.

> "The ecological crisis is not a coincidental feature of capitalism. It is in the DNA of the system. It is not possible to resolve through reforms this incessant hunger, the desire to multiply profits perpetually. The only thing that capitalists can think of when considering the ecological crisis is how much more profit they can make out of it. Therefore, the struggle against the ecological crisis cannot succeed until the capitalist system is removed."

Indeed, the mentality of the solution is important. To create a common ecological mindset in the face of the capitalist mentality that created ecological destruction means to organise and mobilise all of these efforts and bring about a faster and more efficient intervention. Abdullah Öcalan's statement that "the revolution of the 21st century is ecological" not only stresses the extent of the task, but also its importance, as well as the idea that the crisis is indeed resolvable when solutions are implemented. This statement is also important to understand and expose the cleverness of free-market elites and their views that the global ecological crisis can be resolved within capitalism or through reforms. When we look at the effects of the problem on our lives, even if roughly, it is clear that a revolutionary viewpoint and practice is necessary. In order to see this, the problem must be approached in an ethical way; if natural society is the stem cell of the ethical-political society, our perspective on the resolution of ecological issues must contain an ethical dimension:

> "It is not possible to defend the rationality, ethics of any societal system that does not unify with nature. The reason for the system being overcome in terms of rationality and morality is the fact that it is in the greatest conflict with nature. The relationship between the chaos experienced by the capitalist societal system and environmental catastrophe is dialectical. Only the exit from the system can overcome the radical contradictions with nature. It is clear that environmental movements alone cannot overcome this contradictory character. On the other hand, an ecological society necessitates a moral transformation as well. The anti-ethical system of capitalism can only be overcome with an ecological attitude. The ethics-conscience relationship necessitates an empathetic and sympathetic spirituality. This in turn can only carry meaning with a competent ecological equipment. It is friendship with nature, it is the belief in natural religion. As such, it means

to re-unite with the natural organic society, with a new and awakened consciousness. A societal consciousness devoid of an ecological consciousness cannot help but dissolve and corrupt, as seen in the case of real socialism. Ecological consciousness is fundamentally an ideological consciousness. It is like the bridge between the borders between philosophy and ethics. Only if the politics that aim to save us from the contemporary crisis are ecological, can it lead us towards a right societal system."[6]

Perhaps this means to look at our inner mirror when looking for solutions. If everybody turns towards this inner mirror to examine one's own responsibilities, consciousness and actions, ecological problems, and nature's mysterious, extraordinary existence can be felt. With this in mind, we must not allow capitalism to propagate individualist solutions to what requires a global system change.

> **❝**
>
> **No matter how small, there are the remains of natural society in everybody.**[7]
>
> **❞**

**ABDULLAH ÖCALAN**

**Pelşîn Tolhildan** is member of Kurdistan Women's Freedom Party (PAJK) and has been member of the Jineolojî committee for many years.

## NOTES

1. Abdullah Öcalan, 2004, Bir Halkı Savunmak, Devletçi Toplum –Köle Toplumun Oluşumu.

2. Abdullah Öcalan, 2004, Bir Halkı Savunmak, Toplumsal Ekolojiye Dönüş.

3. Ibid.

4. Abdullah Öcalan, 2004, Bir Halkı Savunmak, Toplumda Komünal ve Demokratik Değerlerin Tarihsel Özü, p.95.

Abdullah Öcalan, 2004, Bir Halkı Savunmak, Toplumda Komünal ve Demokratik Değerlerin Tarihsel Özü, p.95.

5. Demokratik ve Ekolojik Toplum Için Bir Taslak (Proje) Düşüncesi.

6. Abdullah Öcalan, 2004, Bir Halkı Savunmak, Toplumsal Ekolojiye Dönüş,

7. Imralı prison island notes.

CAPITALISM CAN NO MORE BE 'PERSUADED' TO LIMIT GROWTH THAN A HUMAN BEING CAN BE 'PERSUADED' TO STOP BREATHING. ATTEMPTS TO 'GREEN' CAPITALISM TO MAKE IT 'ECOLOGICAL', ARE DOOMED BY THE VERY NATURE OF THE SYSTEM AS A SYSTEM OF ENDLESS GROWTH.

MURRAY BOOKCHIN

# AGAINST GREEN CAPITALISM

## Hêlîn Asî

---

In the past few years, movements for ecology and struggles against climate change have gained enormous attention and outreach. The importance and seriousness of the situation, although long known, has been emphasised in recent months by young people around the world. The "Fridays for Future" movements have grown into a notable and remarkably young global mass movement – with local actions in many European countries, Australia, China, India, Japan, Turkey, Rojava, South Korea, Thailand, South Africa, Uruguay, Argentina and Mexico. The weekly strikes are led and organised by young people. The goals are concrete: the fastest possible exit from coal, a complete switch to renewable energies, consistent taxation of greenhouse gas emissions and compliance with the relevant international agreements. Global warming should not exceed 1.5 degrees Celsius. It is now clear to many that these are not unrealistic, utopian goals, but the only way out of the current situation.

## "REZO" EFFECT

In the protests it is made clear that there will be no future worth living if things continue as they have done so far. With similar words, about 100 well-known "YouTubers" launched a call to their subscribers shortly before the European elections, in which they refer to the climate crisis and advise against electing parties that have no prospects in this respect, who stand idly by or even refuse to recognise the crisis. After the enormous success of the Greens in Germany, who were able to double their share of the vote in the European elections, and thus overtook the SPD, commentators now speak of the "Rezo" effect – the YouTuber Rezo had previously published and launched the call. There is no doubt that the climate seems to be one of the most important issues for young people in Germany.

There is a part of society, which should not be underestimated, that continues to deny and trivialise climate change. The climate movements are bombarded with accusations and ridicule. Especially the right-wing, conservative, but also economically liberal, camps try to either deny climate change or trivialise its effects and present it as if the crisis could be solved within the framework of the current situation. The demands of the climate movements are deliberately distorted: it is often said in a scornful tone that the strikers want to go back to the Stone Age, that they would stop "progress" or simply want to skip school under the pretext of a strike. What is certain is that the climate activists must withstand all kinds of delegitimisation. The political right is repeatedly claiming that there are hidden power interests behind the climate movement, and that activists like Greta Thunberg are only puppets in a power game.

## FAILURE OF WESTERN CIVILISATION

It is no wonder that people develop such a vivid imagination when it comes to looking facts in the eye, especially when reality is so at odds with one's own lifestyle, one's own political positions and one's current value and economic system. The climate crisis ultimately reveals the failure of the supposed economic and technological 'progress' of Western civilisation, praised by both liberals and the right. Here I would like to quote the revolutionary, anti-colonialist thinker Frantz Fanon, who said more than 60 years ago:

> **"**
> **For centuries Europe has stopped progress in other people and subjugated them for its own purposes and glory; for centuries it has suffocated almost all humanity in the name of its supposed 'spiritual adventure'. See how today it oscillates between atomic and spiritual dissolution.**
> **"**

**FRANTZ FANON**

The majority are now aware that the neo-liberal system, which is supposedly committed to freedom and progress, has failed at the last. What the exploitation of women workers, worldwide hunger and ever-increasing poverty have shown for decades finds its final proof in the climate crisis. Capitalism has not only uprooted and alienated mankind from (its own) nature, but has also attacked and dismembered nature to such an extent that all living beings are deprived of their livelihood. The climate crisis is not a natural development, nor is it, as some claim, the result of overpopulation.

The climate crisis is the result of unlimited production, unlimited market freedom and a consumerist orientation. It is a question of economic and energy policy, and therefore of the system in which we live. All statistics suggest that climate change is man-made and that greenhouse gas emissions are particularly caused by the excessive use of fossil fuels in the mass production of goods under neo-liberalism.

## NOT ALIGNING THE STRUGGLE TO THE GIVEN CIRCUMSTANCES

It is questionable whether the success of the Greens in the European elections will change anything. Apart from the fact that the Greens did not take any significant steps in the [German] Federal Government in the past, a solution to the current ecological catastrophes cannot be aligned with the given economic conditions. An ecological struggle must be explicitly anti-capitalist and must not make compromises with capital.

The gain of green parties in Europe is therefore not necessarily a gain for the current struggle of the many young people who are working at grassroots level for the climate. On the contrary, the next few years will present the movement with even greater challenges: it must not rely on parliamentary politics and must consistently fight against "green capitalism."

The movements must not bow, and the only way to fight consistently is to develop a positive, socialist perspective for the future, a real alternative that is worth fighting for. The demands and goals should therefore never be formulated only negatively, but should also contain concrete positive answers for a liveable, beautiful future for all. Those who cannot envision an alternative will see no light at the end of the tunnel and will lose themselves in recurring aberrations.

## POTENTIAL FOR A COMMON MOVEMENT

Creating an alternative that brings together and involves all parts of society can overcome an incredible number of barriers. The example of self-governing structures in Rojava/Northern Syria shows the strength of political self-government. People are taken seriously as political subjects and have their say on matters that concern them.

Such a form of grassroots work and organisation is needed so that divisions within society can be lessened. A strongly polarising language is used, especially when it comes to the climate, where 'others' are quickly accused and condemned. But through reproach rejection can even strengthen itself; we must try to win people. Only when people are picked up where they stand and perceived and taken seriously as political subjects in this struggle can a flourishing struggle emerge.

The fact that climate change affects and will affect everyone on this planet without exception can also be seen as an opportunity. The climate crisis has the potential to mobilise all possible movements for a common struggle. Whatever utopias we create, we will not be able to realise them in a broken and destroyed world. The youth of many climate activists is also a great advantage. Children and students whose energies are otherwise exploited and whose rebellions are often punished and subjugated, are now organising themselves and are heard by the whole world. Within a few months, millions of people around the world have risen, even if it all started small.

## ECOLOGICAL STRUGGLE CAN ONLY BE INTERNATIONALIST

"System change not climate change" is what many Fridays For Future protests say. We should take this slogan at its word and organise a way of living together that is worth living for everyone in the world. The ecological struggle can only be internationalist, not only because regional changes are not enough, but also because we have to be aware that the extreme greenhouse gas emissions of the so-called industrialised countries affect above all economically poorer regions, which lack the means to protect themselves from the effects. The supposedly progressive Western civilisation is responsible not only for its own crisis, but also for the degradation of nature everywhere. At the end of history, capitalism shot itself in the foot, and it is now up to young people all over the world to shake off the already broken system for good.

---

Hêlîn Dirik is an activist based in Germany and Italy. She works as a freelance translator and writer with a focus on feminism, philosophy and history. In her German-language feminist newsletter Deng she gives regular updates about current struggles, riots and political events from a feminist perspective.

# THE NEW PARADIGM

## WEAVING ECOLOGY, DEMOCRACY AND GENDER LIBERATION INTO A REVOLUTIONARY POLITICAL PARADIGM

### Viyan Qerecox

I'm sending this message from the liberated territory of the Autonomous Administration of North East Syria, more commonly known as Rojava. I came here over half a year ago to join the work of the revolution and to learn from it. I've been doing ecological works – some tree planting and garden design – as well as working with the women's movement, learning Kurdish and teaching English. Before I came here, I organised with radical groups in the UK for over a decade, including ecological campaigns, feminist and queer groups, the anti-fascist movement and more recently taking a more community organising and radical democracy approach.

One of the main reasons I came to Rojava was because I felt that although there is a lot of amazing organising in the UK, we've also come up against a brick wall in some ways, and we have a lot of questions that we're trying to answer in terms of what kind of world we're trying to build, and how we get there. And when I started to learn more about the revolution in Rojava, I really started to feel that this was a movement that we could learn a lot from, that has, over a few decades, built up something powerful enough to take on the forces of fascism, patriarchy and capitalism, and to establish a society based on ecological sustainability, gender liberation and radical democracy. So, in this talk I'll try to speak a bit about the things that – from the perspective of being here – are the most lacking in the UK radical left movement.

At the root of what we are lacking in the UK, what is stopping us from being able to develop a truly revolutionary perspective, is our inability so far to commit to a new political paradigm that lays the foundation for a different kind of society. Instead, we tend to just react against the most recent outrages that the dominant system throws at us – whether that's fracking, Brexit or Boris Johnson. This talk is being recorded both for the DSEI anti- arms mobilisation, as well as for the Green Earth Awakening, and, at first, I thought it would be really impossible to record something that was suitable for two such different political spaces. But the more I thought about what I wanted to say, what learnings I'm trying to bring from being part of the revolution here, I realised that what was missing in the UK is this common foundation of a new political paradigm, and that's something that we need to build across all the different tendencies and areas of focus within our broader movement. So, although I could talk about how the Turkish state uses both F-15 fighter jets and environmentally destructive dam construction to wage war on the revolution, and I could talk about the ecological projects here – the tree nursery cooperatives, the reforestation of the region, the education systems – I don't think that is what the environmental movement in the UK really needs to hear in order to develop. This awareness and this analysis aren't what we're missing in the UK – we're missing something a lot more fundamental.

In order for the ecological movement – for all radical movements in the UK – to transition from being a movement of protest to a movement of wholesale social transformation, we need a conceptual framework that ties our actions together and gives us a clear direction to work towards. We need to move beyond being anti-fascist, anti-fracking, anti-Boris, anti-capitalist and so on, to being for something that ties together all of our fragmented movements and gives us a common horizon to work towards. One of the biggest threats we are facing as humanity is climate change, and in order to rise to the challenge of organising against a political and economic system whose ideology and philosophy fuels climate change, we need an ideology and philosophy that coherently links together climate change with other forms of oppression. The work of Abdullah Öcalan as well as the philosophy of social ecology have made this link through understanding the relationship between humans and nature as being a facet of the relationships of domination between human and human, and especially the relationship of domination of men over women – what we call patriarchy.

This understanding is a basis, a foundation, of the Kurdish freedom movement's New Paradigm, which was developed in response to the shortcomings and contradictions of a more traditional state-based socialist approach.

The New Paradigm is critical of the institution of the state, seeing it as a mechanism of domination, and instead bases itself on the pillars of ecological sustainability, women's liberation and grassroots democracy. The New Paradigm is more than just an ideology or a strategy, it's a whole way of thinking, of observing, experiencing and analysing, of conceptualising truth. So here we see a bit of a mismatch between what the movement here is proposing as a counter to climate change, versus what our movements in the UK have been able to propose. In the UK, when we talk about fighting climate change, we talk about technology, we talk about legislation and carbon taxes, we talk about rejecting growth-based economics, and sometimes about capitalism. Slowly, more segments of the movement are starting to listen to the voices of communities of colour and indigenous people and saying we need to talk about colonialism, about racism – which is a step in the right direction. In the Kurdish freedom movement, when they talk about ecology, they talk about how we understand truth, they talk about where we came from as humanity, they talk about the knowledge of mothers and grandmothers, of elders. So, this isn't really a talk about ecology in Rojava, this is about the New Paradigm of the Kurdish freedom movement and how it manifests in Rojava and in the ecological approaches of the movement, because you can't really separate it out. The political paradigm of the movement drives the work here, and the insistence that environmental sustainability is intrinsically tied to gender liberation and bottom-up democracy builds a framework of analysis that is a counter-proposal to the paradigm of capitalist modernity, rather than just a rejection of it.

Because the idea of a whole political paradigm is so huge, I find it useful to break it down a little bit into a few different facets. One of the ways I've been looking at it is through three aspects: political culture, ideology, and the democratic system.

So first let's look at the political principles and culture, which for me was one of the most important things to understand. Coming from the so-called 'West', we tend to look at technical, structural solutions to oppression. In terms of ecology, this means trying to change laws, pass international agreements, making renewable technology more available, or banning plastic bags, fossil fuels or high-polluting industries. In wider political organising, even in radical groups, more technical, superficial solutions include building political structures that are more representative, or developing economic systems which are geared towards justice. And before coming here, I would never have called these things technical and superficial, I would have thought of them as structural and getting to the root of the problem. But one thing I have learned here is that we need to go deeper, and my understanding of what 'deep' means is still changing.

To an extent I came to Rojava looking for these technical solutions: how do the councils work? How often are elections? How many people make up a neighbourhood commune? But all of this is completely meaningless without a revolutionary political culture. This political culture has its foundation in trust – in ourselves, in each other, in the ideas of the movement. It's based on commitment and dedication, willingness to give yourself fully – and not grudgingly – to the work that is necessary. To put energy into developing and changing yourself and the people you are organising alongside, rather than rejecting someone if they do something wrong or you don't see eye to eye. It also means giving priority to the collective over the individual, reframing your idea of freedom so that it is less based on individual autonomy and more based on collective liberation. So things like call-out culture don't really exist here. Instead, there is a constant culture of giving criticism with love and respect, because we are committed to helping our friends improve and progress. This political culture, these revolutionary values, are the soul of the movement. Trying to build democratic confederalism – and environmental sustainability – without a foundation of this political culture is impossible.

The second facet is the ideology of the movement. This is as important, or at least almost as important, because it gives a framework and a destination to our political principles. It's through ideology that we analyse the state as a relationship of domination; that we see capitalism as a temporary phase of human history that we can overcome;

that in order to fight patriarchy we need to transfer power to women and other oppressed genders – and so on. I was always really repelled by ideology when I was organising in England, but I feel like I've really connected with the importance of ideology through my time here. Something that is taught here is that your analysis will be wrong if you are working through the wrong analytical lens. And if you fail to construct an alternative analytical lens to the dominant ones – which in the UK are liberalism, capitalism, state-mentality and so on – then you will end up working within the dominant analytical lens. And it's ideology that makes it possible to build this analytical lens. The movement here often explains the shortcomings of Western anarchism and Western feminism in this way – these movements were incredibly powerful, and achieved some great things, but were not able to breakout of the framework of liberalism and therefore got stuck in an individualist, capitalist and state-based way of thinking.

Having some kind of ideology that ties us together allows us to hold the contradictions within our strategy and actions, which is absolutely crucial in terms of fighting climate change. We work in a reality in which it's impossible to fully embody our ecological values in the way that we live, and getting overly fixated on this more lifestylist approach to sustainability cuts off a lot of possibilities to organise on a more collective and fundamental level. In Rojava, the ecological aspect of the revolution has faced countless challenges and is riddled with contradictions. Even though the movement is committed to sustainability, much of it runs off the profits of fossil fuel extraction, the lack of infrastructure means that people burn trash and dump waste, and the embargo means that more sustainable technology is incredibly hard to access. Sometimes decisions need to be made in which a more ecological approach comes into contradiction with a more practical shorter-term approach. However, there is still a principled commitment to ecology that manifests both on a structural level – for example each municipality and region has an ecology committee – but also on the level of ethics, of principles. It seems to me that the lack of this common ideological framework in the UK has meant that we are less able to hold contradictions, so we get really wrapped up in technical debates about plastic straws, or whether to eat vegetarian, local or organic. Although these conversations can be useful, they can stop us from organising more effectively across all of society and building bridges with other radical movements; we develop approaches which can be purist and dogmatic. It means we get stuck in a loop of reactionary politics – reacting against power stations and runways, proposed legislation, or specific politicians – letting these things completely shape our political strategy rather than working proactively to develop a new political paradigm and responding to threats from within that paradigm.

Finally, there are the structures and processes through which the movement here organises. These structures of grassroots democracy and federation build the system of democratic confederalism. This is the more technical element of how the political paradigm manifests in Rojava, and is certainly not a blueprint that can be transplanted from one country to another. In England we will need to come up with our own system of democratic governance, which is shaped by our historical, cultural, social, and economic context. Here, society is organised into democratic units, the smallest of which is the neighbourhood commune. These units federate into district, regional levels and so on, up to the level of the Autonomous Administration of North East Syria. As much power as possible is devolved downwards, so only decisions that have a broader impact are discussed on the wider levels. The system is still very much developing, and in fact not many people thoroughly understand how it works. But – at this point at least – it's being held together by the political culture and values, and the strength of the movement's commitment to finding solutions, addressing mistakes, and putting huge amounts of effort into keeping everything working. And this commitment is at least partly due to the powerful ideology that drives the work and presents a compelling vision that we are all working towards, together.

So, of course, it's not about these three things – political principles, ideology and democratic system – separate from each other. It's the relationship between them, the tensions and contradictions between them. You can't have the organisational structures of the movement separate from the culture and from the ideology. For some people with an ecological background, it might be useful to think of this as a permaculture approach – how we see things as a whole and give meaning to the relationships between different elements rather than breaking them down into binaries:

good or bad, right or wrong, true or false. At the same time as being an ecological approach – because this is how nature works, holistically, rather than through binaries – it is also what would be seen here as an anti-patriarchal approach. And I want to talk a bit more about how the movement connects anti-patriarchy with ecological sustainability – as well as anti-fascism, anti-racism, pro-democracy etc. – because for me this is something that we can really draw on in our organising. And I see a lot of groups in the UK working on developing this analysis and narrative – from the Wretched of the Earth collective, to the Power beyond Borders camp this summer, to the fact that there is an environmentally focused day at the DSEI mobilisation. So, for me, it's about taking that next step and not just linking struggles and making connections, but developing a political paradigm that makes it completely non-negotiable that ecological sustainability, gender liberation, radical democracy, anti-imperialism, anti-racism and anti-fascism are woven together into a movement that presents an alternative to the capitalist paradigm and is powerful enough to take on its power structures.

I've been talking a lot so far on a fairly abstract level, and I'd like to bring some of this to life a bit more. In order to explore what it looks like to build this kind of paradigm shift, I'd like to talk a bit about how women's liberation ties in with ecology and the development of a new kind of society, a new kind of politics. One of the ways women's liberation is being worked for in Rojava is through the development of something called Jineoloji – the science of women. Jineoloji is not a campaign or an ideology, it's being developed as a science, as a methodology, to create a paradigm of analysis and truth that is holistic, rather than breaking everything down into things you can prove, things you can't prove – things that are real and things that are not real. The reason that this is coming from the women's movement is because patriarchy is seen as being tied to a way of thinking that is about binaries, domination, and fragmentation – to the philosophical approach of positivism. Women are seen as being able to hold up a different way of thinking that patriarchy has been trying to suppress for thousands of years, but which has been kept alive all this time through the resistance to patriarchy by women and all oppressed genders. So here again we see the counter-proposal to the patriarchal paradigm, not just a rejection of it. And we can connect it with ecology because the domination of nature by humans goes together with the domination of women by men. And so the leadership of the women of the movement is part of the ecological pillar of the revolution, as well as being part of the democratic pillar.

The revolution in Rojava is a women's revolution. This doesn't just mean that women fought in the armed forces, but that women are taking leadership positions on every level of the revolutionary work. This includes women of all classes, ethnicities, and ages. Mothers are seen as playing a key role in the revolution, and they are often the most radical and bad ass in terms of their dedication, their vision, and their passion. These women don't just happen to be taking leadership positions – the leadership of women is a non-negotiable in the political structures here. All institutions – whether they are community assemblies and local government, cultural institutions, educational academies or political parties – are governed through a "co-chair" or "co-president" system, in which one of the chairs or presidents needs to be a woman. In the context of political representation, this means that a political group that is trying to participate in the democratic system but does not represent women would only ever have one representative in the council, while all the other groups have two. All institutions also have a parallel autonomous women's structure that exists on the same level of power as the general, mixed structure. This is the case from the smallest level – for example a union of teachers in a small town – to the autonomous women's structure for the whole of Rojava – Kongreya Star.

One example of the link between ecology and women's organising is Jinwar, a village set up by the women's movement in Rojava. Jinwar houses women – and their children – who have come together to live collectively and ecologically. The women – who come from different backgrounds, regions, ages and ethnicities – farm several acres of crops, care for animals, run a bakery and collectively manage a shop. Some of their electricity is provided by solar panels, they use ecological farming methods, they are planting trees on their land and they study and share knowledge about natural healthcare. Jinwar brings together the three pillars of the New Paradigm of the movement: democracy, ecology and women's liberation. Other projects – such as women's cooperatives, agricultural projects, academies and community work – do this as well, in different ways. All over North-East Syria, the new paradigm is slowly, gradually, taking hold. It's not easy – it will take lifetimes for the paradigm to fully take root – but it speaks to something in people: our love of freedom, our connection to the natural world, our belief that things can be better.

So how do we do work towards this in the UK? We need to feel ambitious and hopeful. It's really hard to do that while being completely immersed in the reality of life in the UK. Being in Rojava has given me a new sense of perspective, the strength to think big and have political clarity, an ability to think beyond reactionary politics, and the ambition to work towards global democratic confederalism. I would encourage all of you to consider coming to Rojava to join and learn from the revolution here. Through doing this it is possible to experience a new paradigm and open your minds to new ways of organising. It's impossible to describe how it feels to be part of a movement that truly sees capitalism and patriarchy as just a relatively short phase of human history that can be overcome; a movement that is full of people – with all of their imperfections, and mistakes, and struggles – who are giving their lives to building this revolution, day after day.

Last month the Zapatistas announced a massive expansion of their territory in Chiapas with the words "we learned that any dream that doesn't encompass the world is too small a dream." Even from all the way over here, I can see the glimmers of that dream in the UK, and I know that if we're willing to put in the work, we can give it shape. We cannot just limit ourselves to thinking about a single issue, a single area, a single political perspective. We can and must think bigger than that.

I wish you Serkeftin – success – in this work, and look forward to joining you when I return to the UK.

---

This essay is a transcription of a talk – given by a former CFGN staff member in Rojava – recorded in Rojava for the Green Earth Awakening and the DSEI anti-arms trade mobilisation, which both took place in England. The aim of the talk was to highlight the role of ecology in the Rojava revolution, and share lessons that can help build the movement in the UK.

# FURTHER READING

Bookchin, Murray. *Ecology of Freedom*. AK Press, 2006.

Bookchin, Murray. *Philosophy of Social Ecology*. AK Press, 2022.

Bookchin, Murray. *Remaking Society*. Black Rose Books, 1998.

Bookchin, Murray. *The Rise of Urbanization and the Decline of Citizenship*. Sierra Club Books, 1987.

Bookchin, Murray. *Toward an Ecological Society*. Black Rose Books, 1996.

Flach, Anja; Ayboga, Ercan; Knapp, Michael. *Revolution in Rojava: Democratic Autonomy and Women's Liberation in Syrian Kurdistan*. Pluto Press, 2016.

Guneser, Havin. *The Art of Freedom*. PM Press/Kairos, 2021.

Hammy, C and Miley, TJ (2022) Lessons From Rojava for the Paradigm of Social Ecology. *Front*. Polit. Sci. 3:815338.

Internationalist Commune of Rojava. *Make Rojava Green Again*. Dog Section Press, 2016.

International Initiative. *Building Free Life: Dialogues with Öcalan*. PM Press/Kairos, 2020.

Merchant, Carolyn. *Death of Nature, The: Women, Ecology and the Scientific Revolution*. Bravo, 1990.

Öcalan, Abdullah. *Beyond State, Power, and Violence*. PM Press, 2022.

Öcalan, Abdullah. *Capitalism: The Age of Unmasked Gods and Naked Kings*. PM Press, 2023.

Öcalan, Abdullah. *Political Thought of Abdullah Öcalan: Kurdistan, Woman's Revolution and Democratic Confederalism*. PM Press, 2017.

Öcalan, Abdullah. *The Sociology of Freedom*. PM Press, 2020.

Schmidinger, Thomas. *Battle for the Mountain of the Kurds, The: Self-Determination and Ethnic Cleansing in the Afrin Region of Rojava*. PM Press/Kairos, 2019.

# THE INTERNATIONALIST COMMUNE OF ROJAVA

We, as internationalists from the Middle East, Asia, Africa, Europe, America and Oceania, have been working in different structures of the revolution in Rojava and Northern Syria for many years. Though we come from different political backgrounds, the Kurdish movement united and inspired us with a new revolutionary perspective going far beyond the Middle East.

Since 2016 we started to organise as internationalists with the youth movement of Rojava (Tevgera Ciwanên Şoreşger ê Suriyê). In the beginning of 2017, we started the project of the Internationalist Commune of Rojava as a self-organised collective. Today we continue our existence and work in Rojava in coordination with the Revolutionary Youth.

From the beginning our goal was to make Rojava accessible to internationalists from all over the world on an organised level. With the Internationalist Commune of Rojava we wanted to create the possibility to support and learn from Rojava on a social and civil level and create lasting bonds and friendship between the people. To achieve these goals we work based on three principles – 'learn, support, organise.'

We have completed the construction of the Sehid Helin Qerecox Internationalist Academy, and the first terms of education have already been completed there.

In the beginning of the year 2018, we started the campaign "Make Rojava Green Again" together with the entities within the self-administration responsible for ecological work. Several ecological projects have been started in recent years, including the creation of a tree nursery, and we published a book about these works. In 2022, we started our cooperation with the local ecological initiative Keziyên Kesk and will continue on this basis to build ecological alternatives on the ground.

In 2019 we initiated the RiseUp4Rojava campaign. Since then we are organising together with other groups and organisations worldwide to support the anti-fascist resistance in Rojava and on the streets in our home-countries.

Today, members of the commune are working in different structures, learning what this revolution means for the people and for society. We are a part of what is happening here on the ground and as internationalists it is our responsibility to struggle together with the people and to face the multiple threats and challenges together.

## JOIN THE REVOLUTION!

We welcome anyone who has made an effort to understand the principles of the Rojava revolution, and is prepared to come here to learn, support and organise on the basis of these principles.

We are particularly hoping to hear from experienced activists and/or professionals who can contribute to our shared learning process in the projects we are currently working on.

This includes:

- ecological activists, people with experience of permaculture and green/ecological autonomous projects

- engineers, hydrologists, agriculture experts

- language teachers, doctors and other medical personnel, translators

- people with experience of community organising

- people who already speak Kurmanci, or who know Arabic, are of course also very useful here.

What is most important, however, is that people come prepared to learn from the principles of the revolution and challenge their previous conceptions. We need more than just experts – we are looking for committed people with ideals.

## WHAT WILL I BE DOING?

A main principle of ours at the commune is to learn from the principles of the Rojava revolution and the ideas of Abdullah Ocalan, in both theory and practice. When you arrive you should expect to spend time studying the Kurdish language and Ocalan's ideas, and to put these into practice during practical work at the Commune – for example, physical work relating to the Make Rojava Green Again campaign.

In time, most members of the commune will go into society across Rojava to work in different civil structures. Members of the commune are currently involved in projects including the autonomous structures among Yazidi people in Shengal; autonomous women's structures, the women's village, and the Jineology research centres; youth work; medical work; media work; English, art and boxing classes; ecological projects; and the Make Rojava Green Again campaign.

But there is also space here to build and develop your own projects and ideas, in a liberated land free from the repression and constraints of the nation state. If you have ideas for new projects to contribute to our work, we are happy to hear from you.

## HOW LONG SHOULD I COME FOR?

As a rule, you should be prepared to come for a minimum of six months – and preferable longer. This will allow you to learn from the ideology of the movement, improve your Kurmanci and approach the revolution with a long-term and committed perspective.

If this time-frame really isn't possible, do get in touch anyway and we can find a solution together.

## WHAT SHOULD I DO TO PREPARE?

The most important step you can take to prepare is to study the ideas of Abdullah Ocalan and the principles of the Rojava revolution. It is not essential to become fluent in Kurmanci before you arrive, but the more you can learn the easier you will find it to engage with society and the local people and develop a deeper understanding of the situation in Rojava. The day-to-day working language of the commune is English, and education takes place in English or Kurmanci with English translation.

There are also many ways to become involved with the Kurdish movement in other countries across the world, particularly in Europe. If you aren't already, it is very important to find out how you can contribute to the global struggle to support Rojava and spread the principles of the revolution.

## HOW CAN I FIND OUT MORE?

If you've looked at our resources and want to find out more or ask some more specific questions about joining the revolution here in Rojava, you can get in contact with us.

We look forward to hearing from you!

## CONTACT

———————

internationalistcommune@riseup.net

**internationalistcommune.com**

facebook.com/CommuneInt

twitter.com/CommuneInt

## DONATE

———————

Account holder: Rojava Solidarity

Bank account: CH91 0839 0036 9696 1000 5

BIC: ABSOCH22XXX

Bank addres: Alternative Bank Schweiz AG, Amthausquai 21, Postfach, CH-4601 Olten

# THE INSTITUTE OF SOCIAL ECOLOGY

---

The Institute of Social Ecology (ISE) was established in 1974 by Murray Bookchin and Dan Chodorkoff.

The ISE is an independent institution of higher education dedicated to the study of social ecology, an interdisciplinary field drawing on philosophy, political and social theory, anthropology, history, economics, the natural sciences, and feminism. The ISE has offered intensive summer programs, a year-round B.A. degree program, workshops on issues such as biotechnology, fall and winter lecture series, internship opportunities, and a speakers' bureau. In addition, the ISE is involved in research as well as publishing and activist projects.

**social-ecology.org**

## OTHER TITLES FROM
## DOG SECTION PRESS

———————

## MATT BONNER

————

Matt Bonner is a graphic artist, designer, illustrator and campaigner based in London. Matt is co-author of *Advertising Shits in Your Head* (PM Press, 2019) and illustrator of *The Street Art Manual* (Laurence King, 2020), Brandalism's *Subvertising Manual* and *Make Rojava Green Again* (Dog Section Press, 2018 and 2019).

**revoltdesign.org**


## DOG SECTION PRESS

————

Dog Section Press is a not-for-profit publisher and distributor of seditious literature, and a registered worker-owned cooperative.

**dogsection.org**

# DOPE

## MAGAZINE

DOPE Magazine is a quarterly newspaper published by Dog Section Press. Through a horizontal network of distributors around the UK, people ranging from rough sleepers to asylum seekers can collect copies for free, sell them for the cover price of £3 and keep the full proceeds.

DOPE is also free to prisoners, who can request a subscription via Haven Distribution.

Help us to get more DOPE Magazine to more people in more places by supporting our Patreon.

**patreon.org/dopemag**

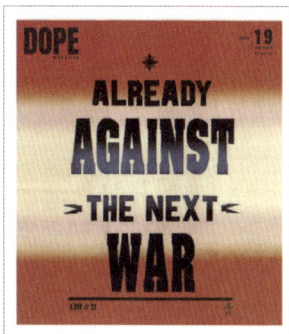

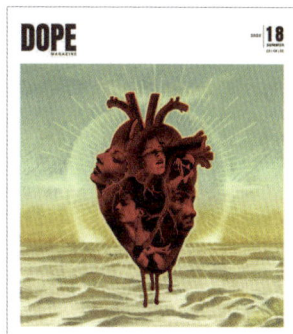

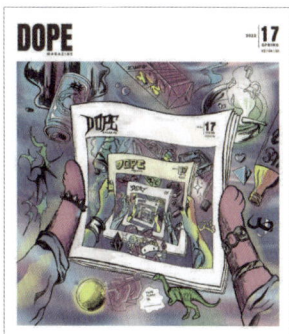

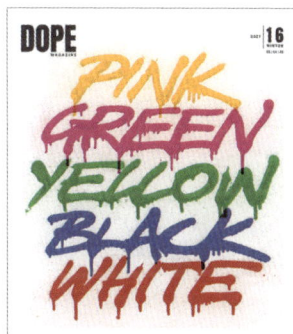

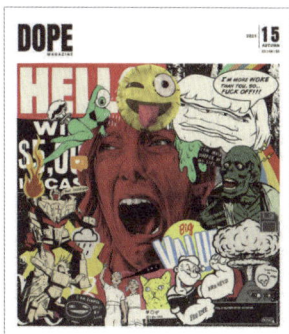

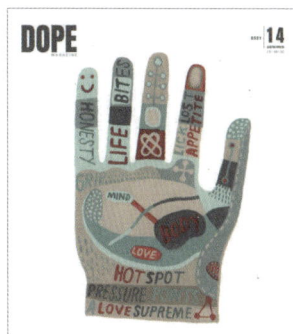